Minds in Motion

Minds in Motion

A Kinesthetic Approach to Teaching Elementary Curriculum

Susan Griss

HEINEMANN
Portsmouth, NH

Heinemann
361 Hanover Street
Portsmouth, NH 03801–3912

Offices and agents throughout the world

The author and publisher wish to thank those who have generously given permission to reprint borrowed material:

"If I Were a Bird" by Edith Segal from *Be My Friend*. Copyright © 1952. Published by Citadel Press. Reprinted by permission of the author.

Library of Congress Cataloging-in-Publication Data
Griss, Susan.
    Minds in motion : a kinesthetic approach to teaching elementary curriculum / Susan Griss.
        p.   cm.
    Includes bibliographical references.
    ISBN 978-0-325-00034-3 (alk. paper)
    ISBN 0–325–00034–4 (alk. paper)
    1. Education, Elementary—Activity programs—United States.
    2. Education, Elementary—United States—Curricula.   3. Movement education—United States.   4. Interdisciplinary approach in education—United States.   I. Title.
    LB1592.G75   1998
    372.19—dc21   97-49593
                                                                      CIP

Editor: Victoria Merecki
Production: Vicki Kasabian
Cover design: Joni Doherty
Manufacturing: Louise Richardson

Printed in the United States of America on acid-free paper

13 12 11 10 09 08   EB   12 13 14 15 16

To my parents,
and
to my teacher and fairy godmother,
Rosalind DeMille

Contents

Acknowledgments

I appreciate that books traditionally include a page of acknowledgments because although writing is a solitary task, the creation of a book really involves many people. This book owes its first acknowledgment to Lawrence Bush, my husband and true partner. It was Larry who originally suggested that I write an article about my work because he wanted to see me spread my wings beyond our immediate community.

After *Educational Leadership* chose to publish my article in 1994, educators from all over the country read about creative movement as a physical language for education. Much to my surprise, letters started coming in from people in nineteen states and six countries—and they're still coming in!

One of those letters was from the acquisitions editor at Heinemann, Leigh Peake. She asked if I would be interested in writing a guide for teachers wanting to use this kinesthetic approach to elementary education. Leigh nursed me along for almost a year, followed by Victoria Merecki. I thank them both for their support and confidence in this project.

As in any profession, I have learned a great deal from my colleagues, among them Livia Vanaver, an inspiring friend, dancer, and educator; Laura Shapiro, who raises my theoretical consciousness and always encourages me to challenge myself; Eileen Wasow, Associate Dean and Director of New Perspectives at Bank Street College; and Mary DiSanto Rose, Chairman of the Dance Department at Skidmore College.

I also want to thank Molly Mason who taught the dance "Galo-pede" at a Hudson River festival in Kingston, New York, and was con-sulted on instructions for this book.

My parents, Doris and Seymour Griss, have always had faith in my pursuits and inspired me to contribute to a better society. I believe the education of children to be an important stepping stone to that better world.

Of course the ideas in this book would not have crystalized with-out the creativity, trust, and joy of the children with whom I've worked over the past twenty years. I am especially grateful to the chil-dren at the W. W. Smith School in Poughkeepsie, New York, and at High Meadow School in Stone Ridge, New York, who grace this book with their photos. Thanks again to Larry for taking those photos, and for guiding me with his editor's eye throughout the writing process.

Finally, a very special thanks to my twins, Jonah and Zoë, for their patience and love while I mothered this book.

Introduction

When I describe my ideas to people about using movement in the classroom to teach elementary curriculum, I usually get two responses. First they exclaim: *"What a great idea!"* Kids shouldn't have to sit behind a desk all day. How wonderful to take advantage of their natural eagerness to move, to express themselves physically. It makes sense that lessons incorporating movement would be fun, memorable, and comprehensible.

Then they ask: *"How in the world do you do that?"* How in the world do you figure out how to teach math, science, punctuation, and so on, through movement-based lessons? How in the world do you permit kids to move around in the classroom without getting out of hand? And how in the world do you get the boys to *dance?*

Minds in Motion is my response. It is my attempt to show teachers how creative movement can be a rich educational resource, and to equip them to use that resource, even if they themselves are not quite comfortable with movement.

For me, the challenge of writing this book has been to make conscious and systematic a technique that I find intuitive. I am by nature and training a dancer and choreographer. Translating ideas and information into movement is something I simply *do.*

"Doing" it as a teacher began for me almost twenty years ago when I worked as an artist-in-residence in the schools. I was asked to work with an elementary class of learning-disabled children in a predominantly Spanish-speaking neighborhood. The first thing I did was ask the principal to schedule a performance date in the auditorium. He didn't want to, he said, "because these children will never be able to put together a show."

Well, with the help of their two wonderful classroom teachers and a beautiful Leo Lionni story called *Swimmy,* we produced an outstanding bilingual dance performance. Children from all over the school wrote letters of thanks.

But there was more to our success, I realized, than the show. Though I'd been hired as an artist to teach dance, the children had learned math as we worked on counts and patterns. They had practiced order and directions. They had sharpened their reading comprehension skills as they discussed and physically experienced the main idea, sequence of events, character development, and conclusions of the story. They had learned about ocean life, and some of them, for the first time, had taken books out of the library. At the same time they developed their coordination and balance and an awareness of shape, timing, and space. This was whole language at its fullest—and to top it off, their self-esteem and creative juices had been thoroughly charged. It became clear to me that creative movement is a powerful classroom teaching tool.

My next teaching experience was in a federally funded program called "Learning to Read Through the Arts." Here I began to structure the *form* of my dance lessons to reflect the *content* of the reading lessons. To learn about main idea we did theme dances: rain dances, planting dances, animal dances. To focus on details we did mirror dances, carefully observing our partners. To understand the importance of sequence we created ritual dances and pattern dances in which the order of the dance was significant. To emphasize drawing conclusions we interpreted Aesop's fables through dance.

In my next job a minor incident triggered a major insight in my work. I was teaching in a gifted program in Poughkeepsie, New York, that offered dance, science, math, writing, and history. I spent four or five weeks with each second-grade group as they cycled through the program. Midway through the term, the math teacher visited me and said, "All the children who have had dance before math are learning the material twice as quickly as those who haven't had you yet. What are you doing?"

I was teaching patterns of movement: A, B, A; A, AB, ABC; AB, AC, AD; etc. The math teacher was teaching patterns in her math class. In my class the children chose their own movements and fit them into patterns, notated them with various squiggles and colors, and performed for each other. We were running, skipping, twirling, laughing—none of us conscious that we were doing a math lesson.

That insight—the interconnection of dance and academics—inspired me to team-teach. I began using the physical language of dance and creative movement to explore concepts and teach information covering a gamut of subjects from environmental science to the U. S. Constitution, from punctuation to molecular theory.

Thanks, in part, to the New York Foundation for the Arts, I have been doing dance residencies in the public schools for many years, including special projects in an art gallery, in a peer mediation program, and with hearing-impaired children. I work primarily with elementary school children, for whom kinesthetic perceptions and responses are much more natural than for older people, who have lost much use of the language of movement. Teaching with this language, I have seen thousands of children develop in affective, artistic, physical, and cognitive areas.

Minds in Motion is a compilation of what I have learned about the techniques, and the magic, of kinesthetic teaching. My goal is to equip and inspire you to develop your own kinesthetic lessons.

If I could have made a painting of all the information in this book, you could see it all at once. Instead, because books are linear, you have to read one part at a time. Feel free to go back and forth from chapter to chapter, and be patient. The more you read, the more insights and techniques will fall into place for you. As you try out some of these creative movement lessons with your students, you will see them integrating their creativity, intellect, and physicality, and you will understand the excitement I feel about sharing my discoveries and expanding my contribution to education through the publication of this book.

EVERY CHILD
WANTS TO MOVE

1

Watch a group of healthy children at play. No doubt they will be moving. Even without hearing their words you will probably know what's going on by watching their activity, their body language, their physical energy dynamics. Children use their bodies to play, communicate, and express emotions. In fact, if you came upon a group of unsupervised children who were not moving (and not watching TV!) you would probably wonder what was wrong.

Children naturally move. They react to and explore the world in physical ways. No one has to teach them to jump for joy, to roll down a grassy hill, or to pound their bodies on the floor during a tantrum. When they arrive in elementary school they are fluent in this nonverbal, physical language. However, rather than using this natural resource by channeling it into constructive learning experiences, teachers often expend energy subduing children's physicality.

What if, instead, teachers used kinesthetic language to teach elementary curricular subjects? What if a second grader's love of spinning could clarify the difference between rotation and revolution? What if a third grader's natural propensity to jump and hop could translate into a lesson revealing the principles of multiplication? What if a fourth grader's excitement about physical adventure could lead into an enactment of a journey on the Underground Railroad, a journey into American history?

When Dr. Howard Gardner identified and described seven areas of intelligence in his 1983 book, *Frames of Mind,* he broadened our understanding of human intelligence beyond the verbal/linguistic and mathematical/logical spheres and brought us closer to a holistic approach to education. While "bodily-kinesthetic intelligence" is recognized as one of our "multiple intelligences," it is one of the most undervalued in our schools. We seem not to understand that learning in a *physical language*—a language that includes kinesthetic activities, creative movement, and dance—is wonderfully natural to most children.

Kinesthetic Learning Is Experiential Learning

Clearly, there are many ways to get information into the brain—by hearing or reading words; by observing; and by experiencing kinesthetically. Proverbs of wisdom from many cultures shed light on the differences among these modes of learning, usually with a marked preference for experiential learning as the richest and most long-lasting. William Glasser estimates the effectiveness of each mode of learning as follows: "We learn 10 percent of what we read, 20 percent of what we hear, 30 percent of what we see, 50 percent of what we both see and hear, 70 percent of what is discussed with others, *80 percent of what we experience personally,* 95 percent of what we teach to someone else" (Bellanca and Fogarty 1991; emphasis added).

In her autobiography, Martha Graham, the grand mistress of American modern dance, offers a related view of the process of education: "[T]he Latin verb to educate, *educere,* indicates . . . it is not a question of putting something in but drawing it out" (1991, 11). Again, through experiential learning, we draw out a deeper understanding of the world in which we live.

Of course, classroom learning must by definition involve a certain amount of abstraction. The classroom is not the world, but ideally a protected, organized environment. Within the boundaries of that environment, however, kinesthetic learning can be far more experiential than chalkboard-centered learning.

The following "science" lesson demonstrates this kinesthetic approach to learning for elementary school children (though college students, graduate students, and elementary school teachers have all had the same response as the children!). Ask the group which medium they *think* sound waves travel through the fastest: air, water, or solid. Most will intuitively respond "air" (thinking of it as less resistant, easier to get through, etc.). Now, have them line themselves up across the floor in three equal groups pretending to be molecules of air, water, and solid. The air molecules stand furthest apart; the solids, closest together. When the first person on each line hears the sound of a single drum beat, they pass the "sound wave"—a shoulder tap—down the line from one person to the next. Of course, the solid group, standing most closely together, finishes first, the air group last.

This activity clearly reveals which medium conducts sound waves fastest; it also demonstrates *why*. It is important to make clear to children that such lessons are not actual scientific experiments (the representation of air, liquid, and solid as lines of differing length is not accurate, although the space between molecules is a definitive component of each medium). Nevertheless, they are kinesthetic activities that graphically and experientially demonstrate scientific principles in ways that young children can grasp and remember. The facts about sound waves will be retained not because children have memorized a piece of information, but because they understand the concept in the most fundamental way. Karen Gallas, in her book *The Languages of Learning*, explains, "I now see, from my own forays into metaphoric thinking about the natural world, that children's thinking reflects a natural ability to express scientific understandings through imagery and analogy" (1994, 72). Children can also *reach* understandings through imagery and analogy.

Indeed, if we subscribe to Piaget's theory that each developmental period of a child's intelligence is built upon the preceding period, we can look for the connections between sensory-motor development and cognitive development. In the period from two to seven years of age, which Piaget calls the "preoperational period," the child begins to conceptualize "through concrete and motor examination of the many dimensions of the external world. . . . This information—derived from the child's active, physical interaction with the environment—provides the data base for building more complex conceptual representations of reality and for supporting the elaboration of these conceptualizations . . . into higher-order, abstract thought processes" (Williams 1983, 13). In other words, young children are processing the world through information they are taking in with their bodies, which later becomes the foundation for abstract thought. This *"action is thought and thought is action"* (13, emphasis added) relationship is quite developed in the early years of elementary school. It stands to reason that during this period children can more easily grasp a lesson that is taught with an active, physical language.

As children age seven to eleven develop through the next stage, which Piaget calls the "concrete operations period," thought can precede action, but children remain secure in their active/physical

DEMONSTRATING A SCIENTIFIC PRINCIPLE

Subject
Relative Speed of Sound Waves

Objectives
I. To enable children to discover if sound waves travel fastest through liquid, solid, or gas
II. To demonstrate longitudinal waves

Time Allotment
20–30 minutes total

Space Requirements
Classroom or larger space

Materials and Suggested Music
Drum, stopwatch, or clock with second hand

Group Format
Whole class working together

Lesson Plan
I. First ask the class through which medium they *think* sound travels the fastest: solid, liquid, or gas. Then set up the following demonstration, on the model of a relay race:

Divide the class into three equal groups—gas, liquid, and solid molecules. Begin with the liquid molecules and line them up one behind the other so that even with their arms extended in front of them, they would have to take three walking steps to tap the shoulders of the person directly in front of them. Then ask if solid molecules are closer together (more dense) or farther apart than liquid molecules. Set the solid group up in a similar line, but let them be close enough so that they can tap the shoulders of the child directly in front without even having to extend their arms all the way. The gas group is then set up the furthest apart from each other so that each person can run several steps to reach the next person in line (the line can curve to accommodate the space). When everyone is set, the solid line closest together and the gas line furthest apart, bang a drum once to signal the last person on each line to pass the "sound wave"—a shoulder tap—down the line from one child to the next within each group.

Children tap the shoulders of the child in front of them, and when the tap reaches the first person of each line, that child yells "solid" or "liquid," whatever their line represents. Of course, the solid group finishes first, the air group last. Again ask them your opening question, and this time when they answer, ask them to explain why. Discuss some of the ways people have used this information throughout history: Native Americans putting their ears to the ground to listen for buffalo or the U. S. Cavalry; listening to the train track to hear if a train is coming.

II. Children line up sideways across the room, shoulder to shoulder about six inches apart, all facing front (pretending to be molecules).

A B C D E F G H I J K L **M** N O P Q R S T U V W X Y

Student M, in the middle of the line, leans to the left and bumps student N. N bumps O, and then rebounds to bump M. (Meanwhile O bumps into P.) Student M then bumps into student L (to M's right), and then rebounds to bump N again. Any time students are bumped, after they bump into the person on their other side, they rebound and bump back the person who originally bumped them (like kids on a lunch line!).

As the ripple of energy (the sound wave) is set into motion, the spaces between students get larger (rarefaction) and smaller (compression) setting up a clear visualization of a longitudinal wave. Just as children will eventually lose their energy to keep on bumping, so too will the sound wave eventually peter out.

This can be done in two groups so children can watch each other.

Children bumping shoulders create the rarefaction and compression of a sound wave

relation to the world. Introducing or reinforcing lessons through a kinesthetic language can therefore greatly assist their understanding of the material.

Creative Movement and Whole Language

Kinesthetic teaching is not meant to take the place of other modes of teaching but rather to be integrated into the curriculum as naturally as speaking, reading, and writing. When we expand our concept of "whole language" to include physical language, we broaden children's access to comprehension. In particular, creative movement—the improvisation of interpretive movements—is an excellent way to engage children with literature. After watching her first graders improvise to the story of *Arrow to the Sun* (McDermott 1974), a teacher reported to a Pittsburgh newspaper that, "she saw an immediate impact on their learning. 'When I asked them to tell me about the story they heard, they recalled more details of the story than they usually do. And they really enjoyed themselves.' "

The story of *Swimmy* by Leo Lionni offers a good example of setting, plot, character development, and theme that can be made accessible and alive to children through creative movement. *Swimmy* is the story of a school of small fish who learn to swim together in the shape of a big fish, to protect themselves as they explore the wonders of the ocean. As the story is read, children will place themselves inside the ocean habitat. They will experience the sequence of events, the tragedies and wonders of Swimmy's adventures, while simultaneously expressing Swimmy's emotional responses. They will feel the surge of collective power as they group together to fool their bigger sea predators.

For many children, such use of their kinesthetic intelligence can clarify principles and information that may elude them in other languages of learning. The following chapters describe lessons that use movement as the classroom language for scientific, mathematical, literary, and historical lessons.

Kinesthetic Learning and Affective Education

Children constantly learn on multiple levels. Fact gathering and other intellectual exercises are only a part of that process. Children are also learning how to interact with others; how they fit into the world around them; who they are; how to pursue and complete projects. They are learning whether or not they think they deserve repect; whether or not they should trust themselves; whether or not they have the ability to succeed. Sometimes we teachers, in focusing on academic learning, overlook these affective outcomes.

Kinesthetic lessons can provide opportunities for a child to learn on many levels besides the intellectual. In a successful kinesthetic lesson, children are learning to make use of their own experiences and observations as a foundation for knowledge. This nurtures self-affirmation and self-esteem because the children's natural resources, their own bodies, are bringing them to a place of understanding.

The first graders who reenacted soil being blown away by a storm, and then repeated the dance, this time adding tall trees whose roots were firmly planted in the ground, were thrilled to discover—when they couldn't roll away—how to reduce erosion. And in a lesson developed by Sue Waters at Marbletown Elementary School, Stephanie, a fourth grader, was excited and eager to identify acute and obtuse angles by bending from her waist—a far cry from the girl who shrank from her teacher's gaze because she was confused by the protractor.

Children can also use kinesthetic learning to explore aspects of themselves that may be hard to reach. By dancing the attributes of wind, from gentle breezes to wild hurricanes and forceful tornadoes, timid children can express their physical power, while aggressive children can find the peacefulness of being soft, of floating. By seeing these hidden qualities emerge, teachers will find their perceptions and expectations of children expanding. Even gender stereotypes get broken down—for wind has no gender!

Giving children the physical and emotional space to explore inner parts of themselves without being told they are right or wrong allows them to integrate their sense of self with the material they are learning in school. The process heightens their self-respect and their school experience, and refreshes their interest in learning. Kinesthetic learning shares the power of all the arts to provide a deep, personal space for exploration of the self and the world—a private space that can nonetheless be shared.

More and more teachers are bringing the arts into their classrooms and lessons by using talents of their own, of specialists in the schools, and of artists-in-residence. Karen Gallas is one such teacher. In her book, she describes many significant moments of learning that are crystalized through a creative process. "Through the arts, teachers and children build an understanding together of how school concepts relate to the child's personal reality" (1994, 118). Without this correlation, learning may seem peripheral to the child. With it, the child's self-knowledge grows with the intellect.

EXPLORING PERSONAL STORIES

Subject
Autobiography

Objectives
To inspire children to express important aspects of their lives

Time Allotment
45 minutes to create dances plus time to show dances to the rest of the class

Space Requirements
Large open space so that many children can work individually at the same time

Materials and Suggested Music
Have on hand a variety of music that children can choose to accompany their dances

Group Format
Working individually

Lesson Plan
This is quite effective for children having difficulty with the written word or for ESL children.

The autobiography will be structured as a kinesthetic song—verses interspersed with a chorus: A B A C A D A E A.

A. Children find a repeatable movement phrase that tells us something about who they are or what they like to do. This phrase "A" is the chorus.
B. Children create movements to show (tell the story of) their earliest memory.
C. Children create movements to show a significant event that happened in their lives (positive or negative) that was *very* important to them and changed their lives in some way.
D. Children create movements showing a family ritual they enjoy that may reflect their ethnicity or cultural background.

E. Children create movements to show a vision of themselves as they would like to be in the future.

Throughout the process, help the children clarify their ideas and their specific movements. Children may choose music for accompaniment and perform their autobiographies for the class. (Performance should be voluntary.) This can be used as the foundation for a written autobiography.

In performance, pay particular attention to the changing qualities which children bring to their A phrase as it repeats throughout the dance, depending on what just preceded it.

Saving Students from Failure

Whatever our form of teaching, we are conveying more than the subject matter at hand: we are encouraging students to develop perseverance, concentration, creative problem-solving skills, order, discipline, observation of detail, imagination, independence, cooperation—the list could go on. These are the building blocks of achievement in any endeavor. Yet when children turn off and drift out the window, they lose it all.

Rodney is a good example. Stumbling through a paragraph that is two years beneath his grade level, his eyes wander out the window to let him escape his frustration and embarrassment. But thirty minutes later, he demonstrates—with confidence and professionalism—the choreography he was taught a week before. Interpreting the nature of the main character in a Dr. Seuss story, he weaves his way from upstage to downstage at the appropriate cue. Adept at this kinetic vocabulary, he helps other slower learners remember their parts. Rodney is developing reading comprehension skills through a kinesthetic retelling of the story. His engagement with the subject matter will also help him stay on task during his regular reading lessons.

By providing alternative paths to subject matter, kinesthetic learning can save some children from the spiral of academic failure. Rather than losing out on the whole learning package, the child who gets distracted or frustrated by traditional forms of teaching can often be motivated and find connections through movement. It's a thrilling experience to see such a child, often in a muddle, coming back to life with focused energy and strong intent. When a child is immersed in the physicalization of a lesson, learning channels open up. Resistance dissipates.

Every class probably has at least one child who cannot stay in his or her seat. A trip to the pencil sharpener, garbage pail, bathroom, or water fountain are the least distracting of the constant occurrences; foot-tapping and falling out of chairs are a bit more troublesome. Yet these children, rather than being a hindrance to the rhythm of your classroom dynamics, can actually heighten the learning energy during kinesthetic lessons. By channeling their disruptive fidgeting into constructive creative movement focused on a particular theme or subject, these very children can emerge as leaders. "[W]hen Brian works through movement and drama," one teacher reports, "the behaviors that handicap him in another situation become his gifts" (Gallas 1994, 138).

These children may not be able to muster the patience to map out a scale drawing of the classroom, but have them convert yards to walking steps, doorways to skips, light fixtures to jumps, and they'll get it. They're moving, their blood is flowing stronger, their oxygen level has increased—so has their interest. It's a lesson gained rather than a lesson lost, and it can fortify them in their next effort to create that scale drawing.

Developing Our Kinesthetic Intelligence

What exactly is bodily-kinesthetic intelligence? According to Dr. Gardner in *Frames of Mind,* "Characteristic of such an intelligence is the ability to use one's body in highly differentiated and skilled ways, for expressive as well as goal-directed purposes. . . . Characteristic as well is the capacity to work skillfully with objects, both those that involve the fine motor movements of one's fingers and hands and those that exploit gross motor movements of the body" (1983, 206). Some people, of course, excel in this intelligence: We know of great athletes, dancers, mimes, musicians, surgeons, and so on. Identifying children who may possess this potential is, in itself, a good reason to introduce kinesthetic teaching in the classroom. However, even if someone does not excel in an area, allowing the development of that part of the self expands his or her consciousness and capabilities and helps to create a "well-rounded individual."

Gardner notes that bodily-kinesthetic intelligence is not widely developed in our culture. Outside of sports, it is not highly valued, especially as a form of expression. In children, kinesthetic intelligence has not yet atrophied; they naturally use it in their actions, explorations, expressiveness, and communication. Is it possible that this area of intelligence is more engaged and accessible when we are children?

The differences between movement workshops for teachers and

movement workshops for children are startling. The kids can't move enough; there are always more volunteers for special demonstrations than are needed; guidance is sometimes needed to limit the risk taking. The opposite is true for the teachers. As teachers, *we actually become role models for limiting kinesthetic development.* We are willing to ignore, resist, and in some cases even condemn this natural, vital language for learning.

The point here is not to berate teachers, but to help break the cycle we unconsciously promote. Later in the book, a chapter called "Not Every Teacher Wants to Move" offers encouraging words and concrete advice for teachers who feel uncomfortable doing movement themselves. The fact is that teachers can verbally lead students through kinesthetic lessons without "getting down on the floor." The children will supply all the movement necessary, with teachers giving direction, boundaries, inspiration, and praise.

Dance and the Creative Process

Apart from supplementing traditional teaching approaches to elementary curriculum, kinesthetic learning can offer children the chance to engage in the creative process through dance. As in the creation of any art form, choreography—making formal and aesthetic decisions to create a dance that can be repeated—calls upon and develops a multitude of skills.

The creative process of choreography leads children to develop the germ of an idea through many stages of brainstorming and exploration, analysis and synthesis, refinement and editing. Discipline, persistence, and the ability to be organized and to take risks are general requirements for success. More specifically, students must embark on a journey to gather "information" about a subject—facts or feelings, externally derived or personally intuited.

As the raw material grows, students must choose pieces of it to further develop and explore making connections and discovering new pathways and insights. Soon a shape begins to form from the material. Now students must choose what to discard as redundant or unnecessary, as they tighten and define the work. Finally, usually after some constructive criticism, the work is fine-tuned or refined, and students are ready to present in public, with dignity and ownership, a creation that they have helped to birth. Throughout this process, children working individually or with a group learn powerful lessons about leadership and cooperation, conviction and compromise.

Of course, not all teachers have the ability to guide children

CHOREOGRAPHING A BOOK REPORT

Subject
Book Reports

Objectives
To physically express the elements of a book report: the theme, sequence of events, aspects that were significant to the reader, character development

Time Allotment
Varies

Space Requirements
Large open space if the whole class is working together

Materials and Suggested Music
To be chosen appropriately for each book

Group Format
In small groups or individually

Lesson Plan
The class can be divided into small groups to work on each section, or a small group or one person can do the whole piece. The dance should show the theme of the story, possibly as a repeating theme in the dance to divide different sections. Parts of the story in their proper sequence can be performed, showing aspects of the emotional life of the main character. Attention should be paid to a part of the book of particular interest to the reader, i.e., a special relationship between two characters, an unusual character, a dynamic event, the setting of the place or period. Music can be added to provide a mood or quality rather than as a formal structure to which the dance would be choreographed.

Working in this mode may necessitate "rewrites" prodded by inspired questions from the facilitator.

The final piece can be performed for the class, with a chance for the audience to ask questions and make comments.

through the creative process in the medium of movement. Dance is an art form in its own right and should be presented with integrity by an experienced artist. But in this era of arts-in-education institutes and artists-in-residence, every school has access to dancers and choreographers with whom teachers can collaborate. This *team* approach brings out the best that artists and teachers have to offer.

By providing children with a physical language to experience the creative process—a process which some cannot access through the written word—we can deepen their cognitive development. In fact, the cognitive skills identified in Bloom's Taxonomy (which many teachers use in developing lessons) parallel the creative process. Knowledge, comprehension, application, analysis, synthesis, and evaluation are all integral to the creation of art.

When we provide our students with these expressive skills, whether verbally or through another medium, we are empowering them as individuals. When we engage them in the creation of group projects, we are empowering them as a community.

A New Way of Seeing Each Other

In our society and in our schools, there is much talk about respecting diverse cultures. Dance, perhaps the oldest art form of human expression, is a particularly compelling way for children to explore and experience both the universality and the particularity of those cultures. By learning ethnic dances and physically interpreting poetry, literature, and folklore, children develop insights into the aesthetics and value systems of other lands and other people. Including multicultural dance in the curriculum also offers an opportunity to invite professional artists—and parents—to share their expertise with children in the classroom.

Kinesthetic learning can also address issues of diversity as they arise between individuals. We are, for example, always receiving visual messages from one another's body language—messages that elicit responses of respect, fear, attraction, intimidation, trust—yet we rarely acknowledge these messages or engage openly in bodily conversation. *Bringing physical language into the classroom offers children a rare chance to* look *at one another, to see each other, and learn how to show respect for each other's differences in a nonthreatening arena.* Kinesthetic learning encourages an acceptance of difference because no two people have the same bodies or move alike. When it comes to self-expression, moreover, there is no "right" or "wrong" movement. Just as teachers discover hidden dimensions in their students by watching them move, so can children learn about each other. The constructive intimacy that arises from such observation is a wonderful asset in any classroom.

Conclusion

For teachers concerned about educating *the whole child,* kinesthetic language can open many doors. Dance, creative movement, and kinesthetic activities nourish growth in cognitive and affective realms of development. Kinesthetic teaching makes subject matter accessible by concretizing the abstract. It involves children in the creative process and develops higher-level thinking and social skills. It provides an affirmative means for self-expression. If you follow the maxim "Teach from the known to the unknown," you will understand the value of allowing children to learn from their bodies.

Each elementary school child feels, experiences, *knows* his or her own body. By affirming the worth of this self-knowledge as a pathway to other knowledge, we can encourage children to take risks, to explore new territory, and to respect and trust themselves. Their learning will be manifold.

FROM MUSCLES TO THE BRAIN
Dissecting a Lesson

2

So you've decided to do a kinesthetic lesson. How do you choose a topic that will lend itself to a kinesthetic approach and ensure that this class time will be educational, successful, and fun? For starters, look for topics that offer at least one of three points of access: (1) the possibility for creative interpretation; (2) kinesthetic elements, for instance, motion, time, space, shape; (3) authentic dance forms. The following sections will help you identify and use these points of access.

Creative Interpretation

The first point of access, creative interpretation, is probably the easiest for a person untrained in dance to identify and use to develop a kinesthetic lesson. Any subject that involves some sort of drama or emotion can probably be interpreted through movement by the children. Trust your intuition. If you can imagine your students acting out a story or situation without having to use words, you probably have an appropriate lesson.

You will supply the narrative by reading or telling the story as the children move. The more comfortable you feel moving as you recite the story, the more easily children will adapt to creative movement. Be careful, however, that they don't copy everything you do. Ideally, you want them to discover their own movement vocabulary.

Stories about nature (wind, oceans, animals), about work people do (farming, building, hunting), or about adventurous journeys, all lend themselves to movement improvisation. The more motion in the story, the better. Through movement, the children will experience the sequence of events, the action, the interactive forces in the story, the physical setting. Concepts like "main idea" or "cause and effect" become more accessible.

As a general rule, rather than choosing different children for different parts, allow everyone to do everything. That way, each child will experience all the aspects of a story, just as the reader of a book does. In the Leo Lionni story *Swimmy*, for example, all the children can be Swimmy at once, even though they are swimming alone in the "deep wet world . . . scared, lonely and very sad." A good exception to this rule is when there are two clear opposing forces, as in Aesop's fable *The Wind and the Sun*. Here it is helpful to allow children the dynamic interplay between the elements.

Movement interpretation offers children a way to climb inside history—to understand historical situations and current events in a dynamic and personal way—which inevitably stirs deeper interest and thoughtful questions. Children studying the Underground Railroad can crouch behind imaginary rocks and trees, race across fields at midnight, jump from one ice floe to another, carry an injured friend into a cornfield to hide, and rest on their journey to escape from slavery. Children studying current events in the Middle East can create tableaux (people sculptures) depicting the yearning, fear, distrust, and hope of the Israelis and Palestinians. A series of these tableaux can be very effective to show changing relationships of power.

Poetry that depicts motion or emotion can be entered through a physical doorway, especially by younger children. Dancing the natural world—falling leaves, free-flying birds, swirling snow, pounding buffalo—or human experiences—fear, aloneness, giggles, friendship—can make poetry more tangible for them. For more sophisticated fifth and sixth graders, creating dances to poems written by Bosnian children who are living through a nightmare of war can provide a sensitive and personal way to approach a difficult subject. Performing for other classes can stimulate thoughtful peer discussions.

Even creative writing can be enhanced through movement. Emotions of anger, shyness, fear, and loneliness can be experienced through physical improvisation by the writer so that his or her descriptions become more nuanced and subtle. Something as simple as monster dances, animal dances, or autobiographical dances can help writers move beyond generalizations into specific details. Words like "nice" or "scary" or "happy" or "sad" can be given shape and texture through movement. By physicalizing their imagery, children will find the words

CLIMBING INTO HISTORY

Subject
The Underground Railroad

Objectives
To provide children an engaging way to learn about the Underground Railroad

Time Allotment
45 minutes

Space Requirements
A large open space is preferable, though with modifications, it can be done anywhere

Materials and Suggested Music
July 1984, *National Geographic Magazine; Follow the Drinking Gourd* by Jeanette Winter, published by Knopf, Inc., NY, 1988; old spirituals about freedom, especially *Follow the Drinking Gourd*. Also two wonderful tapes:

> All for Freedom
> Sweet Honey in the Rock
> Music for Little People MLP 2230
> PO Box 1460
> Redway, CA 95560
>
> Music and the Underground Railroad
> The Kim and Reggie Harris Group
> Ascension Records KRH 002
> Box 18871
> Philadelphia, PA 19119

Group Format
   I. The whole class together
   II. Divided into smaller groups

Lesson Plan
I. After teaching a history lesson about the Underground Railroad, (there are excellent pictures and stories in the July 1984 issue of

National Geographic Magazine), turn out the lights, play spirituals on the tape recorder and meet the children in the corner of the room. You get to play the role of Harriet Tubman or any other conductor on the Underground Railroad. Wait for everyone to finish each leg of the journey before starting a new movement. Encourage students to help each other along the way, and to stay quiet so "you don't get caught." A possible scenario:

Describe an imaginary house up on the hill, and a low wall between you and the house. Lead the children along a path so that you have to bend low behind the wall in order not to be seen. Run in a large circle as if you are running through the field as fast as possible to get away from the plantation and barking dogs.

Sneak through the woods by hiding behind trees every five feet so there's not too much movement in the woods to attract attention from the road.

Cross the icy stream at the edge of the woods (so the dogs lose your scent) by stretching from one stone to another. Be sure not to get your feet wet or they could get frostbitten from the cold.

Point up to the Big Dipper constellation and use it to find the North Star to guide you northward on your journey.

Someone gets a foot caught in an animal trap. After it is released by smashing the spring with an imaginary rock, have the person carried to a nearby cornfield. Someone else may be carried for fatigue.

Crossing an icy stream on the Underground Railroad

Dawn is coming. Instruct everyone to take a nibble of bread and a few sips of fresh water. This is a safe field and you can sleep here for the rest of the day. You will wake the group as soon as the sun starts to set.

II. Divide the class into smaller groups of about six or seven children. Have them create and perform their own scenario of a journey up north on the Underground Railroad. The journey should include some mishaps and how they are overcome as well as a variety of terrains. Also each group can decide if they want one leader, alternating leaders, or if they want to make decisions as a group. Students may choose to be specific characters including family members.

to describe the monster slashing its gigantic claws, or the little girl curling her body into a ball of sadness. The process of going back and forth from moving to writing (or talking) can thus enrich vocabulary and make language come alive.

It's worthwhile to note that in every example of creative interpretation given above, no movement is *necessary* on the part of the teacher. While a teacher's movements could guide and inspire students, her primary role is to provide the structure of the lesson, the physical and emotional space, and the verbal guidance to help children analyze the experience. The children will always supply movement. See Chapter 5 for further discussion about this topic.

Kinesthetic Elements

Does a topic have a relationship to motion? time? shape? space? Are any of these elements of dance essential to the central understanding of your lesson? If so, you've got a topic that's appropriate for a kinesthetic lesson. Think about your own ways of describing the topic. Look for action words, words describing force, shape, direction, sequence, or timing. Science topics are prime candidates. For example, the lesson described in Chapter 1—"through which medium do sound waves travel fastest, solid, gas or liquid?"—was triggered by the words "travel," "wave," and "fastest." "Travel" and "wave" tell you immediately that motion is involved; "fastest" implies the kinesthetic element of time. The word "medium" is also a clue: children can demonstrate physically the differences in density—that is, space— among a gas, a liquid, or a solid. From these key words, the structure of the kinesthetic lesson took form.

Motion

You may wish to choose only one aspect of a subject, such as motion, to explore or emphasize through movement. When teaching about magnetism, for instance, you can make use of the fact that *attract* (opposite poles) and *repel* (like poles) are *motion* words. The children can create group dances in which students moving on the same level (high or low) must move away from one another, and students moving on different levels must come toward one another. This may seem a rather involved way to teach a relatively simple

UNDERSTANDING BODY SYSTEMS

Subject
Systems of the Body

Objectives
To allow children to physically experience the workings of the I. Circulatory, II. Digestive, and III. Nervous systems

Time Allotment
Each lesson approximately 20–30 minutes

Space Requirements
Large open space

Materials and Suggested Music
    I. About twenty-four feet of string or fabric
    II. 2 or 3 five-yard pieces of fabric (coat lining is great)
    III. Bowl of water
Symphonic music can be used for all three

Group Format
Whole class as one group

Lesson Plan

In general, students will use their bodies to reenact the process of a particular body system, traveling the complete path of blood, digesting food, or being part of the nervous system transmitting messages to the brain or to muscles.

I. CIRCULATORY SYSTEM. Indicate on the floor where the heart would be (approximately 4' × 4') and the lungs (each approximately 4' × 6') on either side of the heart. They may be drawn on the floor or outlined by string or fabric. The rest of the space will represent the rest of the body.

Two children stand in the heart (left and right sides) directing and "pushing" the blood in the proper direction; the rest of the class becomes the blood (high level movements—i.e., arms high, walking on tiptoes—in the arteries carrying oxygen; low level movements—i.e., bent over, arms toward the floor—in the veins carrying carbon dioxide). The teacher will explain and/or demonstrate the entire circulatory process before the whole class begins.

IN THE ARTERIES: Blood moves along a path doing high movements with other blood in a group (like a highway). Gradually disperse the group into separate paths (like country roads) maintaining high movements but slowing speed.

IN THE CAPILLARIES: When each child is alone, he or she should gradually lower the level of the movements (giving up oxygen) and continue to slow down. At the lowest level begin a path back toward the heart.

IN THE VEINS: Team up with other low level movers headed for the heart, keep a slow tempo.

IN THE HEART: When the blood enters the upper right chamber the right side heart child pushes it gently to the lower right chamber, and then pushes it harder to the lungs.

IN THE LUNGS: Enter lungs and do a low swinging movement with an exhaled breath. Inhale with a high movement and continue doing high movements back to the heart.

BACK TO THE HEART: Enter upper left chamber and get pushed gently by the left side heart child to lower left chamber, and then pushed harder out of the heart. Doing high level movements (oxygenated blood), follow the paths through the body to continue the cycle.

II. DIGESTIVE SYSTEM. Using long cloth (2 or 3 five-yard pieces of fabric) to represent the food, have the children act out the different parts of the digestive system using their *whole* bodies. Children are arranged in two facing lines either standing or on their backs. Allow a few extra yards

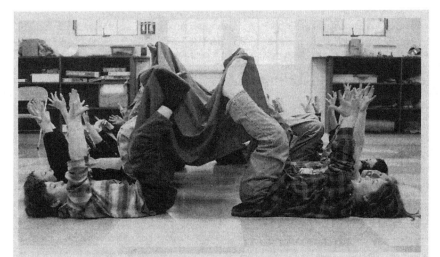

With extended arms and fingers as villi, children reenact the small intestine during digestion

of cloth to extend past the first children so they have enough to pass down. Everyone can do every part to understand the whole system:

TEETH—chewing motions with hands, arms, and legs

SALIVA—with fluid quality, move bodies with cloth

PHARYNX and ESOPHAGUS—pass cloth down the double line of children in small pushing movements of contraction and release

STOMACH—churning, mashing, and mixing movements

SMALL INTESTINE—children lying on backs with legs passing cloth (chyme) down the line, arms and fingers waving in the air (villi)

LARGE INTESTINE—fluid movements passing and throwing cloth away from group (excretion)

III. NERVOUS SYSTEM. Similar to teaching the other body systems, re-create the nervous system using students to represent the different parts. Pass messages by squeezing hands or passing other "impulsive" gestures (rippling through one arm, into the torso, and out the other arm) and flick (spray) water from fingers to cross over the synapse between axon and dendrites. Different stimuli could travel on different pathways to the brain, so that some students could be sight, some sound, some touch, etc.

concept, but it has three advantages: (1) kinesthetic learners are immediately engaged and involved in the content of the lesson; (2) children who learn through their muscles viscerally remember information that they might otherwise forget; and (3) the kinesthetic understanding of magnetism lays the foundation for understanding how electricity works.

A different aspect of motion can be physically explored in the digestive, circulatory, and nervous systems of the body. With the class becoming one body going through the *motions* of the particular body function, children can help figure out how to show the difference between blood carrying oxygen (e.g., high level energetic movements) and blood carrying carbon dioxide (e.g., low level, sluggish movements), or how to show an impulse being passed between the axon and the dendrites in the nervous system.

Another aspect of motion is force. Force may produce motion, change direction or speed, or prevent motion if two opposing forces are equal, as in children finding a balanced shape by pulling away from each other while remaining connected. Kinetic energy, simple machines, and even the concept of checks and balances in the U. S. Constitution involve force.

Time

Time not only involves the speed at which something happens, it can also involve duration (lasting through time), transformation (changing through time), or sequence (ordering in time). The cycle of plant growth from seed to seed, the water cycle, the metamorphosis of a butterfly, the cycle of seasons, or math patterns can all be taught kinesthetically.

Another way to view time is through rhythm. Clapping and moving the rhythm of spoken language is a very successful way to teach syllables. Arithmetic fractions can also be seen as rhythm: half notes, quarter notes, eighth notes. Children can practice their fractions through rhythmic movement: 8 runs (8 eighths) take the same time as 4 skips (4 quarters) or 2 body swings (2 halves). The movements can also be put together as mixed fractions in phrases of equal duration (measures): 2 runs and 1 skip plus 2 runs and 1 skip equal 4 runs and a body swing, or 8 runs. Children can create their own movements and combinations.

Which subject *uses* the word "time"? Multiplication. The magic of multiplication can actually be experienced by children through movement. The twelve skips of four children each doing three skips one after the other takes a certain amount of time. But ask those same

MULTIPLYING THROUGH MOVEMENT

Subject
Multiplication

Objectives
To help children understand the concept of multiplication as a physical process and to practice multiplication

Time Allotment
15 minutes

Space Requirements
Small area is okay

Materials and Suggested Music
Lively, rhythmic music

Group Format
A small group at a time with the rest of the class observing

Lesson Plan
I. To demonstrate multiplication: 4×2
Have two students stand together. Add two more, two more, and two more until there are four pairs. Count the total number of students standing.

To demonstrate the concept of multiplication: 4×3
Four students stand next to each other. They are each going to do three jumps. Let's count how many jumps altogether while they jump one at a time. (The first student jumps one, two, three; the second student jumps four, five, and six; the third jumps seven, eight, nine; and the last jumps ten, eleven, twelve.) That was like adding $3 + 3 + 3 + 3$ to get 12. If we want to see how multiplication works, let's have the children do three jumps each but at the *same time*. Ready, set, go! How many jumps did we see altogether? Did it take as long as when they did it one at a time?

II. Ask students to do three jumps with a partner, first one at a time $(3 + 3)$, and then together (2×3). How many jumps did you and your partner do together the first time? The second time? Which demonstrates multiplication?

Five students take 4 backward steps one at a time $(4 + 4 + 4 + 4 + 4)$. How many backward steps in all? Now they do it at the same time (5×4). How many backward steps in all?

Have the children create their own demonstrations and compute the equations.

children to perform their skips *at the same time,* and you see the twelve skips in condensed time: $3 + 3 + 3 + 3$ becomes 4×3.

Space

Kinesthetic teaching is perhaps most direct in the realm of space. Space refers to three-dimensional space (height-width-depth), to paths created traveling through space, and to the space between objects. For young children, physical and directional concepts can be kinesthetically experienced: large, small, diagonal, tall, wide, front, side, back, near, far, over, under, through, behind, spiral. For older children, kinesthetic lessons can clarify the difference between revolution and rotation or between clockwise and counterclockwise; relationships of planets and other heavenly bodies within the solar system; the density of molecules in gases versus solids; the process of evaporation; the density of gradations of rock (sand, silt, clay, gravel); the overcrowded and inhumane conditions of slave ships; the study of maps and scale; and arithmetic division (twelve can be arranged in space as two groups of six, four groups of three, twelve groups of one, etc.).

Shape

Shape as a kinesthetic element becomes most obvious when teaching art and design, symmetry and asymmetry, letter and number shapes, and geometry—subjects we associate with shape. But it creeps unexpectedly into other topics. Studying punctuation, children can "walk" through sentences and use their whole bodies to create shapes that represent the appropriate punctuation marks. Drilling long and short vowel sounds, children can make long/tall shapes for words like "huge" and short/low shapes for words like "hug." (The fact that children will be influenced by the responses of others around them should be seen as a positive means to learning, not as "cheating." See

Chapter 4 for further discussion about using such activities as tools of assessment.)

The accessibility of shape as a kinesthetic element, even for very young students, makes it especially good for giving information (bats rest hanging upside-down), stimulating associations (create the shape of a rainforest animal), or directing the focus (make the letter shape of a vowel) at the beginning of your lessons. Shape can also provide a transition to the more subtle element of motion: "Make your body into a shape that is round" (or long, or sad, or proud, or a cat, or a bird). "Now move in that shape." This process of joining shape to a locomotor movement helps inspire more creative detail in movement "across the floor" and expands a child's movement vocabulary.

The creation of motionless group shapes, called tableaux, can also be a very expressive learning experience. They may be done singly as a statement, or in a series to show states of transition within a cycle (as described in the section on time). Creating sculptures made of still, posed bodies, children can depict a scene from a story (for example,

An abstract tableau using multiple levels and shapes

GROUP SHAPES: CONFLICT RESOLUTION

Subject
Conflict/Feelings Tableau

Objectives
To help children identify feelings and separate feelings from action

Time Allotment
     I. 15–20 minutes
    II. 20–30 minutes

Space Requirements
Open space

Materials and Suggested Music
I. Cards with a different emotion printed on each one

Group Format
     I. Groups of eight to ten
    II. Groups of four

Lesson Plan
I. After warming up with a freeze game on the subject of emotions, group the children in circles of eight to ten, sitting on the floor. Place a stack of "emotion" cards face down in the center of the circle. Each child chooses a card and nonverbally acts out the feeling on the card while the rest of the circle guesses what emotion is being expressed. (Synonyms should be accepted.)

II. Divide the students into groups of four. Ask each group to create a simple scenario of a conflict that ends in a fight. Explain that a tableau is a grouping of people frozen like statues to create a scene. Ask each group to create a tableau expressing the conflict: Two of the students will assume poses relating to each other, showing the fight; the other two students will assume poses behind or next to each of the fighters showing the feelings that are underlying the anger (hurt, fear, embarrassment, etc.).

Hurt and fear underlie the anger of this posed fight

Each group presents their tableau to the class, which tries to identify the feelings and the scenario.

Let the students discuss how they could resolve the conflict if the fighters were removed and only the *feeling* people remained.

Rosa Parks being asked to give up her bus seat to a white person), a moment of transition (the metamorphosis of a butterfly), or relationships between people or characters (a situation in which some children represent a conflict and other children represent underlying feelings). Tableaux are best made in groups of three to five children, using various shapes on differing levels, to be viewed from all perspectives like a sculpture in a park. Consciousness of symmetry and asymmetry may be included as an element.

Authentic Dance Forms
The third point of entry for creating kinesthetic lessons is authentic dance forms, which can augment the study of literature or history to reveal deeper dimensions of diverse cultures.

Performing a Native American round dance, for example—focusing on its relationship to the earth, its sense of timing, its significance as a circle—can deepen children's awareness of certain spiritual values within Native American culture. Similarly, the rhythms, energy, and individualized styles of Appalachian clogging, with its roots in Irish, African, and Native American dance, provide a visceral insight into the diversity of early American culture.

These are lessons to be taught by guest artists, but it is the classroom teacher who can bring it together and help the children analyze what they are learning. Exposing young children to other cultures through dance and music expands their understanding of a pluralistic world in which difference is respected and universality is celebrated.

Strategies for Developing Kinesthetic Lessons

Once you know which of the above points of access are to be found within your subject matter, you will know in which direction to take your lesson. Since all subjects are not necessarily suited to a kinesthetic approach, clarifying the specific point of access will help you determine whether to get involved in movement.

Simply stated, you want the children to experience or express kinesthetically whatever you are studying. If the topic involves emotion, have the children feel and express the feelings. If it moves, have them re-create the movement with their bodies. If it involves time, have them experience the timing. If it involves space, have them physically describe the spatial relations. If it has shape, have them create the shape with their body, alone or as a group. If it involves another culture, have them experience elements of that culture through dance.

Children are generally not afraid to take on other identities. They are eager to be animals, molecules, wind, machines, even different personalities and characters. Perhaps it is part of discovering who they really are; perhaps it is an affirmation of their limitless imaginations. Whatever the reason for children's willingness to enter this kinesthetic theater, teachers can use the energy as a great resource for learning.

Keeping your lessons simple and specific will ensure success for you and the children. Sometimes choosing only one part of a lesson to teach kinesthetically is enough to capture the students' interest and clarify a concept.

The projected outcomes of your lesson can help you to choose an activity. The following examples will help guide you.

OUTCOME	KINESTHETIC ACTIVITY
Reading comprehension	*Improvise to a story*
Learn a sequence or progression	*Order movements and floor patterns to represent the history of transportation, or use gestures and levels to represent the water cycle*
Analyze the mechanics of a process	*Exaggerate the vibratory motion of molecules passing a sound wave*
Make observations	*Compare two experiences: Did you need less energy to run directly up a two-and-a-half-foot-high platform, or up a ramp that led to the platform?*
Learn facts	*To represent Venus, spin clockwise. Spin counter-clockwise to represent the other eight planets*
Show what they know	*Use shape and motion to show three characteristics of your animal*
Synthesis	*Using African rhythms, create a group Harvest Dance based on the seven principles of Kwanzaa*
Express something personal	*Dance your earliest memory*

As you are drawn to specific subjects for kinesthetic lessons, you will discover that many subjects can involve more than one creative movement element. For instance, a lesson on the speed of sound waves can involve motion, space, and time. A lesson on the Underground Railroad can involve creative interpretation, motion, space, time, and authentic music and dance. A lesson on a story like *Swimmy* can involve interpretation, motion, space, and shape. Ask yourself what you want the children to learn from the lesson, then choose kinesthetic elements to bring home that learning.

Kinesthetic teaching reflects the natural language of children. As you give them permission to "speak" this language in the classroom, your students will amaze you with their abilities to interpret, express, and analyze ideas through movement.

3   STRUCTURING THE LESSON
Space, Control, Time, and Format

Once you have a sense of the lesson you want to teach, you need to present it in a manner accessible to your students. The space, time frame, and format you choose will affect the success of your lesson. Remember that it took time for you to develop the techniques you now use to be an effective teacher. Be generous with yourself and your students as you learn which kinesthetic methods work best. The physical quality of kinesthetic teaching will help by giving you immediate feedback.

Space
Having the appropriate space is one of the most important requirements for teaching a kinesthetic lesson. Imagine asking children to play musical instruments in a library where they have to be quiet, or in the noisy cafeteria at lunchtime. Asking children to dance in a cluttered room where they have no space and are bumping into each other is a set-up for frustration. Children need space to move.

It is possible to use your classroom for certain kinesthetic activities if the desks are pushed back. Children can also take turns in smaller groups in the classroom and even in the hallway. But ideally you want to work in an open, uncongested space such as the gymnasium, cafeteria, or outside in warm weather. Children need a *clean* area free of obstacles and diversions. Use your own judgment. If you would not feel comfortable moving in a particular space or sitting on a particular floor, chances are at least some of your students will feel the same way. Respecting their need for comfort lays a good foundation for your working relationship.

After the space is chosen, define its boundaries. Children need to know where they can move and where is off-limits. It may take practice for some children to stay within a defined area when they are joyfully engaged in your kinesthetic activity. A few friendly reminders can serve to keep the peace and maintain the pace.

Control

Once you are in your work space, be very clear about your expectations: you are here to *work* rather than play. For children, moving bodies and open space generally translate into play and noise unless you guide them in a different direction. From the beginning, establish a nonverbal method to get the children's attention and to stop all motion and sound. A strong drum beat works very well. Clapping a rhythm and having the class echo the rhythm is more fun but more gradual. Stopping the music or turning off the lights can be helpful, but are not captivating enough on their own. A loud command like *"freeze!"* is always a good accompaniment to whatever you choose. Having control not only facilitates the lesson for you as a teacher but also gives the children a sense of security. They will be more willing to explore new areas if they know you are holding the reins securely.

Allow children to practice what it is like *not* to bump into each other. With younger children, try describing an invisible bubble or protective shield around each child that is impenetrable. Make a game of how close they can move around each other without touching—fast and slow, high and low. Contrast the movement with moments of stillness signaled by your drum (or whatever you use to call the children to *freeze*). This is an enjoyable way to reinforce respect for each other's space.

Time and Format

Each lesson should have its own structure with a warm-up, a development, a culmination, and a closing. In general, a half-hour class works well for kindergarten, forty-five minutes for first through fourth grades, one hour for fifth and sixth. Of course the specific children and the specific lesson will influence your time allotment, but these time frames work well for most classes.

The younger the children, the more they respond to repetition and ritual. For kindergarten, first, and second grades, having routine openings (warm-ups) and closings (warm-downs) are useful to help the children digest the experience and pace themselves.

Beginning/Warm-up

For all ages, each session should start with some nonchallenging group movement to warm up the participants both physically and emotionally. Moving as a group will provide a feeling of safety and lessen the opportunity for distracting behavior. Beginning with a circle, in which everyone is connected and can see everyone else, gives the group a cohesive, egalitarian feeling. The group's energy is more palpable and contained in this formation and can be better directed. In a smaller space, an inner and outer circle can work. As a third option, you can have the class spread out, all facing you. Whichever format you choose, make sure that everyone has enough room to swing arms and legs without bumping into a neighbor or furniture.

Most of the lessons you teach will not require an extensive physical warm-up. The warm-up serves to engage the kinesthetic part of the brain through nonpedestrian movement (movement not ordinarily experienced during the course of a day). This, in turn, helps open doors to more creative physical language.

The warm-up should focus students' awareness of their body, the space, and other people in the space. You may choose to warm up different parts of the body by swinging, rotating, flexing (bending), and extending—the four possible ways our bodies can move. Or you may prefer to focus on movement qualities, ranging from very large, outgoing movements to small, subtle movements; from fast movement to slow motion; from movements with tense muscles to loose, free-flowing movement; from laying on the floor to reaching way up high—even jumping off the ground. (Caution: no jumping until the legs and feet have been warmed up!) Of course, a fabulous musical accompaniment is a must! Rhythmic, "friendly" music provides energy, support, and structure to help focus the children.

Singing a simple opening song that describes the warm-up movement is very inviting to younger children. You can make up your own melody or put new words to a familiar tune. Changing the timing from slow to fast adds a fun surprise and keeps them alert. Here are two examples of songs we sing in a circle:

Hello Sky

HELLO SKY

Hello sky way up high,
Let us reach up to the sky.

Swing our arms round and round,
Bend down low and touch the ground.

Side to side we sway and bend,
And say hello to all our friends.

Reach to the sky, touch the ground,
Love our friends who are all around.

Tick Tock

TICK TOCK

Reach our arms up high
Curl up and get low
Stretch up tall narrow as an arrow

Reach out wide from side to side
Tick Tock Tick Tock   *(rock back and forth)*
Round and round and round and round we go.
                                    (spin and freeze)

Reach our arms up high
Curl up and get low
Jump up tall narrow as an arrow
Jump out wide from side to side
Tick Tock Tick Tock   *(rock back and forth)*
Round and round and round and round we go.
                                    (spin and freeze)

Reach our arms up high
Curl up and get low
Wiggle up tall narrow as an arrow
Press out wide from side to side
Tick Tock Tick Tock   *(rock back and forth)*
Round and round and round and round we go.
                                    (spin and freeze)

These songs describe motions or shapes that the children will perform, but the actual movement is left up to the individual child. There are no right and wrong positions. So long as the children are following the directions of the song they will have immediate success.

Freeze Game

Part of the warm-up may also introduce the content of your lesson, so that the warm-up evolves around a theme. The Freeze Game is a simple and fun way to introduce theme. Children move around the space doing any locomotor movements they choose, and *freeze* whenever the signal commands. While they are quiet and in a frozen position, direct them to do the next freeze in a shape related to your lesson (i.e., an animal, a letter, an emotion, an aspect of the ocean, a high-level shape).

The children can also use your direction to guide their locomotor movements: How would you move if you were in a weightless environment? Seaweed in the ocean? A hawk searching for dinner? Blood filled with oxygen?

EXPRESSING FEELINGS WITH THE FREEZE GAME

Subject
Emotions

Objectives
To help children identify and express feelings

Time Allotment
10–15 minutes

Space Requirements
Open space

Materials and Suggested Music
Drum

Group Format
The whole class working together

Lesson Plan
Ask students to name aloud all the feelings they can list (worried, excited, sad, angry, shy, embarrassed, depressed, confused, etc.). Discuss the ways we show our feelings nonverbally such as through eye focus, facial expression, gestures, posture, and muscle tension.

Call out a feeling, and ask the children to make a body shape that reflects that feeling when you bang the drum once. After a moment, ask the children to *move* how that emotion *feels,* and accompany the movement on the drum. When the drum stops, the children freeze. Repeat this sequence with a variety of feelings. Instruct the children not to make any sounds or touch anyone else during the exercise, but to focus their attention on the changes they are making in body shape, muscle tension, and whether they feel open or closed.

Groupings and Development
From kindergarten through second grade, children do well with guided movement to perform specific activities: dancing to a poem or story as it is being read aloud; using body parts to form a letter of the alphabet; demonstrating number values through rhythmic movements;

showing the qualities of different intensities of water, wind, or fire; depicting a natural cycle like the water cycle. They may work well moving individually but within a group, or with partners. Specific movements will be chosen by the children, but you will lead them through the content and variations using your voice as a road map: "Now let's do it high, fast, upside down . . ."

With older children, start by directing them through a lesson in which you are the constant guide. Then allow them to apply, analyze, or synthesize the information by working on their own in small groups to create movement pieces. Remember, they will require clear directions as to the structure of the assignment. These are projects in which the children use the elements of dance—time, shape, space, and motion—to personalize and more fully digest what they have just learned. The groups may range from two to five children.

You may also ask these children to create static tableaux depicting the correct sequence and content of your subject; or to create a piece in motion showing a process of change with a clear beginning and end; or to come up with a new example of something they are studying. Be explicit in your instructions: Show three different ways that; Create your own movements using the same pattern as; Show the five stages of; Create a new ending to the story about; and so on.

While the children are working in their groups, circulate and ask questions to guide them: Have you chosen your opening shape? Which cycle will you demonstrate? In which direction will your audience be sitting? Or ask to see what they have created so far. Each time they show you some work it will encourage them to clarify their ideas, set their movements, identify what is missing.

Culmination/Showing Work

For children working on dance projects, it is beneficial to have at least one group perform their work-in-progress for the rest of the class before a session ends. This establishes accountability on the part of the performers and provides a way for the whole class to evaluate an example of the process in which they, too, are engaged. This can also be a time for inspiration and brainstorming, and another chance for the teacher to articulate the method and goals for the lesson.

Giving children—even young children who are improvising and not concretely setting their movements into choreography—the chance to observe each other's work is a valuable experience. This need not be done as solos. Three, four, five children, or even half the class, spread out in the space, can present their work simultaneously. Whether you structure this at the end of the session or somewhere in the middle, you are sending a vital message to each child that her or his work is worth viewing, and you are setting up a level of expectation for the child to fulfill. Children will learn from their observations that there are many ways to solve the same problem. They will also learn how to be brave performers and a respectful audience, and how to give and receive constructive criticism.

If older children are to continue working on a project over a period of time, they need to have a sense of accomplishment at the end of each session. Showing a work-in-progress is one way to meet this need. Groups can also pair off, showing works informally to each other at the end of a work period, or each group can take a few moments to write down what they accomplished that day. These notes may be a combination of words, drawings, sketches of floor patterns—anything that will help them remember their creations.

The longer the process, the bigger the culminating goal has to be to sustain the energy. A planned major performance with costumes and an invited audience can sustain a few months of work. Otherwise, three to four sessions should be considered an extended project. Keep most lessons to one or two sessions to keep a good momentum going for the children.

Endings

Just as the freeze game can introduce the lesson for the day, the closing can be structured to review briefly what just happened in class. This is a closing kindergarten song we do in a circle. The children create body shapes in response to the words they sing:

(Everyone Sings)	(Teacher Says)
Today we were open,	*Remember when we . . .*
Today we were closed.	*Remember when we . . .*
We stretched through our fingers,	*Remember when we . . .*
And down to our toes.	
Today we were giant,	*Remember when we . . .*
Today we were small.	*Remember when we . . .*
We felt very little,	*Remember when we . . .*
We felt very tall.	*Remember when we . . .*

We made shapes that were low,   *When we . . .*
And middle,   *When we . . .*
And high.   *When we . . .*

And now it is time
To say our good-bye.

Closings are an important transition. If the children finish a lesson feeling overstimulated and hyperenergetic, they will have a difficult time focusing their attention on the next aspect of their day. For older children, regrouping in a circle, breathing deeply while doing large, stretching movements (reaching tall) and releasing (drooping to the floor with knees slightly bent), or verbally reviewing the main points of the lesson, helps to ground their energy.

Variety

As with any method of teaching, variety will help engage the students in your kinesthetic lessons. You can teach poetry one day and math another. You can do a short science lesson and an extended project on Greek mythology. The whole class can work together as a group learn-

Improvising with silk scarves

ing about density and individually exploring a specific emotion or memory. Groups can be duets, in which two students balance each other's weight, mirror each other's movements, or contrast each other's levels. Groups can involve three, four, or five students. (Depending on the activity, listening and cooperating may be very challenging for five children working together.)

Varying the music also brings new energy to your teaching. Music can set a mood and a tempo, unify the class, and provide gentle boundaries. It can also help generate a kinesthetic response from children who are having a hard time motivating themselves around a particular idea. (See Appendix II for a list of suggested music.)

Props offer yet another element of variety and stimulation. Hoops can be used to define space (inside, outside, above, below, through). Silk scarves can encourage fluidity and motion. Elastic can focus attention on movement quality and shape. Balloons, kept aloft with head bobs or shoulder thrusts or knee kicks, can help isolate body parts. Yards of colored fabric can help create an environment. Sticks, hit against each other or the floor, can highlight rhythm. The list could go on indefinitely. The key is to use props to *extend* body movement, not replace it.

Creative Movement for Classroom Management

Not only is it important to keep control during kinesthetic lessons, but kinesthetic activities can actually help you with classroom management during the regular course of a day. Here are some tried-and-true methods for using creative movement to help children focus when they seem noisy and out of control.

- Clap out a rhythm. Then point to the class, to clap the echo of your rhythm—even if only a few children notice you. (If they don't understand what you want, pantomime what they should do.) Repeat this procedure a few times until a bunch of your students are doing it. Then change the rhythm each time you clap, so that the children have to listen to what you are clapping. After a few turns, the whole class will be fully attentive to your every beat, trying to copy you. When you're ready, stop. They'll be ready for whatever you have planned.

- Find a catchy rhythm that is long but easy to remember. Punctuate it with claps, snaps, or slaps on the thigh, and teach it to your students. Whenever they hear you do the rhythm, they are supposed to join in and stop what they are saying or doing. Have a flashy ending that signals a freeze and silence, like a fist in the air or a final stamp. Believe it or not, this really works. Even if you have to do it an extra time through, it saves you from screaming louder than your students, and turns what could become an angry interaction into a positive experience.

- Another way to focus attention is a game called "Who's Sharp Today?" created and taught by Sherye Weisz, a faculty member of Lesley College. This one works well in a circle and needs quiet to begin, but engages distracted children.

    Start by saying, "Let's see who's sharp today. When I bang on the drum, put your hands on your head." Then bang the drum once, and the children will put their hands on their heads. Next say, "When I bang on the drum put your hands in the air." But this time only begin the motion of hitting the drum, and stop midway. Some if not all of the children will have their hands in the air. When they realize they went too soon and return to their heads, *then* bang the drum and have them put their hands in the air. You can make this game as complicated as you want: Put one hand on your knee and the other on your elbow; use two hands but hold up only five fingers; point down and look up. You can also pass the drum to different students and have them make up the directions. It's hard to resist focusing with a game like this.

- Here's a simple way to transport your class from one area to another (from seats to the story rug; from activity centers to seats) without having them fall apart. Any variation will be fine: *If you're wearing yellow, you can skip over. If you have laces in your shoes, hop to your seats. If your birthday is in the summer, swim across. If your name has three syllables, tiptoe to the mat.*

- Another way to bring the group into a circle sitting on the floor is to sit in the circle and begin to play a hand rhythm hitting the floor, clapping, snapping, tapping head and shoulders, etc. The children will gravitate over, just to join you in making music.

- When entering a new space, you can have the children follow you single file and play follow the leader, copying your movements. Or you could lead them in a geometric floor pattern (an oval, diamond, triangle, etc.) and have them guess which shape they just walked.

Putting It All Together

Planning a kinesthetic lesson is not all that different from planning any creative work project in the classroom. It is mostly a combination of good teaching skills, common sense, and familiarity with the medium—which you can acquire only by getting your feet wet. Start simply and grow with your students.

The similarities between kinesthetic and traditional teaching are basic. Every classroom lesson has its own rhythm, with an introduction and a conclusion. Sometimes children work alone, sometimes in pairs, sometimes in groups. Activities have to be timed—between lunch, gym, recess, library, art, music, and the other hundred activities in modern public schools. And there's never enough space!

A kinesthetic lesson differs from a traditional lesson in its language—a physical language with its own syntax, subtleties, humor, and connection to the brain. It is all at once an everyday language that children recognize and the language of an art form with its own particular rules, elements, and nuances. It is a universal language with many dialects and is an effective tool for learning.

4 ASSESSMENT
Evaluating the Mind in Motion

Kinesthetic activity, a powerful teaching tool for a wide variety of subjects, can be equally powerful as an assessment tool—a ready means of perceiving a student's understanding of specific subject areas. Such an assessment process will be valid, of course, only if students are familiar with kinesthetic language and fluent in it. The more immersed your classroom is in kinesthetic learning, the more apparent the benefits of kinesthetic assessment will be. In a kinesthetic activity, a child's understanding of a specific subject is *immediately visible* to the teacher. Teaching and assessing can therefore be integrated, and the distinctions between learning and "testing" can be diminished.

Later in this chapter, you will find a range of activities that can increase your students' kinesthetic fluency and equip them for a kinesthetic assessment experience. But first, explore some of the "ways of knowing" that can be assessed through kinesthetic activity. The discussion that follows is built upon the widely used *Taxonomy of Educational Objectives* (Bloom, 1984 reprint).

Cognitive Assessment Through Kinesthetic Activity

Knowledge
A physical response to your questions enables you to see which students have not yet grasped information you want them to *know*. For instance, in assessing their understanding of parts of speech, you might direct your students as follows: "If the word is a noun, make a still shape; if it's an adjective, move without traveling; if it's a verb, travel."

As you ask about specific words, you will see pretty quickly who is sure or unsure about the answer. If this does not become clear while watching the whole class, try having them move in groups of five or six.

This is one example of kinesthetic assessment for "category-type" knowledge. Almost any knowledge that can be expressed through shape-and-motion assignments can be assessed—as long as you offer a clear contrast between response choices. High and low, fast and slow, right side up and upside down should all evoke clear responses. (Be careful with choices that may be similar, such as left and right. These can easily be mixed up and mislead your assessment process.)

In the example above, the directions for classifying the parts of speech make sense: the still, stationary shape for a noun; the descriptive but nontraveling activity for an adjective; the traveling action for a verb. Your kinesthetic assessment activities, no less than your kinesthetic lessons, should be rooted in the subject matter and expressive of its truths, rather than simply arbitrary. In this way, assessment, too, becomes an active learning experience for students.

Comprehension

To assess comprehension, you might ask children

- to create body shapes that show you a sequence of events in history
- to use body movement to demonstrate three encounters that a character had in a story
- to portray the water cycle kinesthetically.

These are dynamic, fun alternatives to classroom discussion, and may well invite the classroom participation of the less verbal or less focused child. Kinesthetic assignments allow children to translate or explain something in their own language (in this case a physical language), and allow teachers to see whether students have really digested the information they are now retelling.

Application

Kinesthetic assignments can be very fruitful for assessing how students are applying information and insights that are being taught. After studying certain rules of punctuation, for example, a student should be able to create sentences and physically express the punctuation marks. When assessing students' abilities to transfer directions from a two-dimensional map into three-dimensional space, you might have

ASSESSING MAP LITERACY

Subject
Maps

Objectives
 I. To help children transfer information from a two-
    dimensional map to three-dimensional space
 II. To assess whether children can create a map describing their
     floor patterns and movements, and to assess whether
     children can kinesthetically read a map

Time Allotment
 I. 20–30 minutes
 II. Approximately 45 minutes

Space Requirements
Large open space

Materials and Suggested Music
 I. Prepared maps, any music
 II. Paper, colored markers, any music

Group Format
 I. Groups of two to four children
 II. Pairs

Lesson Plan
Preparation: Using colored markers, create maps of floor patterns for
children to follow in a given space. Supply a legend of colors and symbols so they can decipher which movements to do as they follow the
outlined path. For instance, a curved line of red *x*'s may indicate skipping in a curved path; a dotted purple line going to the corner may indicate running to the corner; a squiggly green spiral may indicate
walking in a spiral; and so on. Be creative—children can go backward,
sideways, leap, hop, jump, spin, and more!—but limit each map to four
or five directions.

I. Divide children into groups of two to four, and give each group a
map to follow. Let them decipher the maps by going through the

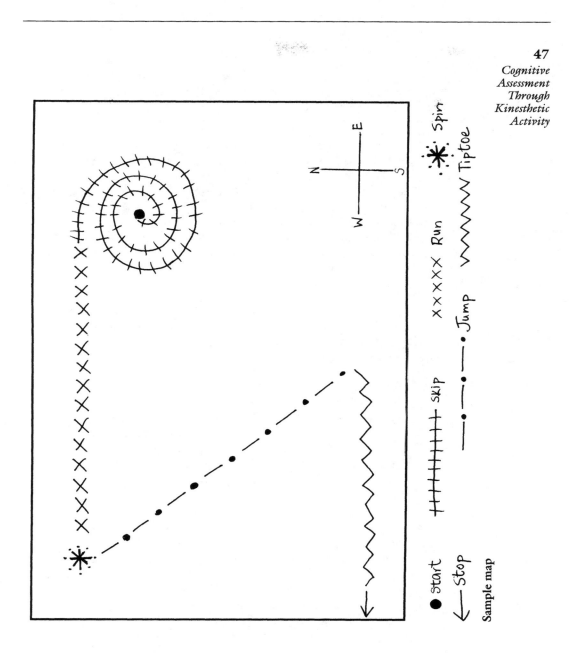

Sample map

actual motions in the space. When they can do the path without look-ing at the maps, let each group perform their path. Two and three groups can then perform at the same time if you know they won't crash into each other.

II. Using colored markers and paper, let each child create an original map for a given open space. Instruct them to create the movements in the space first, and then to draw the map with a legend of colors and symbols. Children then exchange maps with a partner and try to follow the movements and floor pattern drawn by their partner. When they can perform without having to refer to the maps, children can perform for the class. After each one, have the student show the map. The class can comment on how well the map was drawn and in-terpreted.

them move through the space deciphering the floor patterns (where to travel) and symbols (how to travel) from a map which you've created. Then students can create their own movement patterns, which they re-create as a map with colored markers using original symbols. Other students could then try to follow these student maps.

Analysis

To see how a child analyzes a subject, you can ask the child to choreo-graph a transformative process—for instance, a seed growing into a plant and reproducing itself through its own seed. Older students might create a series of tableaux showing the emotional relationships of characters in a story, or choreograph a dance examining both sides of an historical or social issue, such as Manifest Destiny and the West-ward Expansion.

Synthesis

Assignments designed to assess a student's ability to synthesize mater-ial may be among the most creative of all, for synthesis is, by definition, a creative process in which knowledge, comprehension, application, and analysis of a subject combine to produce an original creation. After studying the African American holiday Kwanzaa, for instance, students can choreograph a dance with African steps and rhythms, revealing the seven principles of Kwanzaa. After reading an autobiography, students can choreograph solo dances expressing the perspective of the author. When studying immigration, children can choreograph a dance showing the experiences of the immigrant from arrival through assimilation. When studying astronomy, students can create a dance showing the patterns of our solar system. Through these creations, details can emerge, perspectives and relationships can be revealed, cause and effect can be seen.

In all of this, it is important to remember that assessment is valid only if the student is familiar and fluent in the language of the assessment. For the kinesthetic learner, the activities suggested above can be very successful and reveal subtle insights that may not be apparent in a written or verbal assessment process. However, for children who have never choreographed a dance before and who may have difficulty expressing themselves through creative movement, this would not be a valid form of assessment. Allowing children the option of choosing a kinesthetic form of assessment respects their differences, recognizes their strengths, and makes them active participants in the assessment process.

Tools of Assessment: The Elements of Movement

Increasing a student's control of the medium increases the scope and detail of what they express. The more you teach kinesthetic lessons and expose children to the tools of kinesthetic expression, the more nuanced and daring their responses to your assignments will be. You can help them gain this fluency by guiding them in the following exercises. These could be done as part of your warm-ups or freeze game, in the course of your lessons, or simply as relaxation or skills-building activities.

Children can move to a variety of *rhythms and tempos* by improvising to a wide range of music or by dancing to their own timing. They can practice fractions by dancing to the rhythm of a waltz (thirds) or a march (quarters), or to fifths, sixths, sevenths, and so on. Students can echo each other's rhythms by clapping and then *moving* the rhythm: one student can clap the rhythm, then the partner moves it, or a student can move the rhythm first, then the partner will clap it. They can have rhythmic conversations, one making a nonverbal, rhythmic statement (clapping, stomping, moonwalking, nodding) while the partner listens, then responds. As the conversation unfolds, the dynamics and lengths of statements should vary and be responsive.

To experiment with the use of *space*, children can explore various floor patterns such as straight lines, diagonals, spirals, squiggles, zigzags, and curves. Direction can be changed from front to back to sideways; focus can be shifted in, out, up, or down. Bodies can be arranged—close together or far apart—in different group designs such as a circle, line, wedge, semicircle, clump, and so on.

Body *shapes* can be explored as symmetrical or asymmetrical; balanced or off balance; low, middle, or high; rounded, angular, cavelike, extended. Number and letter shapes can be practiced; environments can be imagined and moved ("Let's make the shapes of things that live in the ocean"); character and emotion can be explored ("Let's make the shape of the girl being scared; of the friend being worried").

Children can create an infinite number of ways to travel across the floor (*locomotion*) based on walking, running, leaping, sliding, galloping, hopping, jumping, and skipping. Imagining how various animals move will inspire many new ideas, and so will imagining different terrains such as hot sand, slippery ice, mucky mud, a rocky mountain, or gravity-free outer space.

Combining elements with one another introduces more complex creative possibilities. Jumping (locomotion) can become jumping backward in a circle (locomotion and space), or jumping in a zigzag pattern from a low, angular crouch (locomotion, space, and shape). Running diagonally can become running in slow motion, building up speed, climaxing with a high jump and tight shape in the air, and landing in a roll along the ground to the corner.

Choosing a specific *movement quality* adds another dimension to these activities. Performing a movement with tight, resistant muscles is very different from performing it with loose, free-flowing energy. The same is true for movements that are percussive (jerky) versus sustained (smooth), strong (pressing) versus light (floating), or direct (moving straight) versus indirect (meandering). Each choice expresses a different *feeling* that can be stimulated by a specific circumstance—being chased, leaving a place you want to stay, escaping through barbed wire, arriving on an unknown planet. By helping children investigate these possibilities you are increasing their kinesthetic vocabulary, which expands their potential for expression—and your potential for a meaningful kinesthetic assessment.

Tools of Assessment: Structuring the Movement

There are many ways movement can be structured to help students express themselves kinesthetically. Previous chapters have mentioned *improvisation, choreography, journeys, conversations, gestures,* and *tableaux* as formats that children can use to communicate. Each of these formats will, in an assessment process, reveal different levels of reflection and information.

Improvisation means moving creatively without preplanning the movement. You may set an open structure (move the way you feel; dance to the music; act out the story as it's being read; explore one image in the poem through movement) or you may set specific guidelines or rules (if you're the same magnetic pole as your partner, move away from each other but stay on the same level; if you are opposite, move toward each other, but on different levels). What marks this as improvisation is that movement emerges spontaneously. No one knows what will happen until it happens.

Choreography, while it might incorporate improvisation to stimulate movement ideas, involves planning, creating, editing, and remembering. Choreographed movement can be performed over again because the performer knows in advance what the movements will be. Students can choreograph a dance on any theme. However, the more specific your guidelines, the easier the task may be for some children. At the very least, a choreographed dance should have a beginning, a development, and an ending; it should use the elements of movement to communicate a feeling or an idea; and its parts should be integrated into a whole.

A *journey* literally starts in one place and travels to another. There may be a traveling theme—a step or movement that recurs—and events can happen along the way. A journey may take the form of a song with verses and a repeating chorus, performed with movement rather than sound. A timeline or sequence of events can be demonstrated clearly if you use this format. In a kinesthetic book report, the theme can be expressed as a movement chorus, and the plot and characters as different movement verses. Though movement is the main medium for a journey, the use of spoken words to highlight or explain a section can be acceptable and even encouraged. Together, the movements and words may communicate more than either can alone.

Conversations are movement dialogues involving two or more people, each reacting to what others have just stated. Students can use this format to show the relationships among characters in a story, among nations, or even among ideas.

Gestures are movements of at least one body part (usually limbs) that do not travel across the floor (nonlocomotor). Because gestures are stationary, they can be performed at a desk in the classroom. For instance: Show three ways fire can be used today that are similar to 1,000 years ago; create a pattern using four gestures, then use the gestures in an accumulation pattern (A, A B, A B C, A B C D); describe the water cycle.

USING THE TABLEAU

Subject
Symmetry/Asymmetry

Objectives
    I. To help children understand the concepts of symmetry and asymmetry; to help children decipher symmetrical and asymmetrical components of larger shapes
    II. To reinforce children's knowledge of the life cycle of the butterfly; to provide an opportunity for children to apply their knowledge of symmetry and asymmetry

Time Allotment
    I. 20 minutes
    II. 30–45 minutes

Space Requirements
    I. Classroom is fine
    II. Small open spaces for groups to work

Materials and Suggested Music
    I. Optional: Five photos of a body posing in a symmetrical shape; camera
    II. Photographs of the metamorphosis of a butterfly; optional: gentle classical music

Group Format
    I. The whole class together
    II. Groups of six students (five or seven can work with a modification)

Lesson Plan
I. Demonstrate or show pictures of five symmetrical body shapes without identifying them. Try to vary the shapes so that one is high, another low, one has bent limbs and another straight limbs, one faces front and another back, etc. Ask the class what each of these shapes has in common. (You may have to give some hints after a while.) When the class recognizes that they are all symmetrical, ask each student to create

Combining symmetrical and asymmetrical shapes to form a symmetrical tableau

a symmetrical body shape. Repeat on different levels. Create asymmetrical shapes the same way.

Once the students are clear about the difference between symmetrical and asymmetrical shapes, ask a student to come in front of the room and create a shape that is asymmetrical. While that student holds the asymmetrical shape, ask another to join the first student *as if they were one statue or tableau,* so that the new combined shape is symmetrical. (For instance, if the first student is facing the class with a bent left leg and an extended right arm, the second student will have to face the class with a bent right leg and an extended left arm, to make the tableau of the two students symmetrical.)

Ask a third student to add a new shape to the existing tableau, maintaining the symmetry of the whole shape. (The third student would have to create a symmetrical shape placed right in the middle of the other two students, either in front of or behind them.)

Next ask a fourth student to make a symmetrical shape, but add on to the tableau so that it becomes asymmetrical. (This shape would be independently symmetrical, but placed on one side of the tableau.)

Finally ask a fifth student to add one more shape, making the tableau symmetrical again. (This student would have to do the same symmetrical shape as the fourth student, but on the opposite side of the tableau.)

If you have a camera, you can take a picture of the tableau before it disbands.

II. After studying the stages of the metamorphosis of a butterfly, divide the class into groups of six (five or seven can work too). Referring to pictures for details, have each group create four tableaux showing the stages of metamorphosis (egg, larva, chrysalis, butterfly). Instruct the students to use symmetrical and asymmetrical shapes within symmetrical and asymmetrical tableaux in the following way:

GROUP TABLEAU SHAPE	INDIVIDUAL BODY SHAPE
asymmetrical	symmetrical
asymmetrical	asymmetrical
symmetrical	symmetrical
symmetrical	asymmetrical*

*If there is an odd number of children in the group, one will have to be symmetrical.

Students can decide which tableau will go with which stage of the metamorphosis. Make sure students are clear about what is "front" when performing the tableaux, so that dividing a symmetrical tableau down the center line will have mirror images on either side. Using a variety of levels will also make the tableaux more interesting and creative.

When the four tableaux are choreographed and rehearsed, the children can try adding slow transitional movements to get from one shape to the next. Music can help tie the piece together.

After each group performs its dance, allow the rest of the class to discuss what they saw in terms of content and form.

Tableaux are statues, or stationary shapes, formed by groups of people. Done in a series, tableaux can tell a story or show a sequence of events. They are described in Chapter 2 under the section on shape, which is their strongest element. Because a tableau is made of more than one person, it can reveal a range of details, highlight power relationships, and show the relationship of parts to a whole.

Each of the movement formats described above offers children an opportunity to express their ideas nonverbally. It also gives them a chance to experience and evaluate their ideas through a different medium, which may provide a new perspective. Often, surprising details emerge from this physical language, details that otherwise might have remained unobserved or unexpressed.

Self-Assessment/Group Critique

Students are accustomed to being graded by their teachers, and generally have little input into the evaluation process. Kinesthetic presentations offer the opportunity for students to learn how to be self-reflective, and how to evaluate each other's work—invaluable skills in any field of endeavor. Having the chance to evaluate their own and each other's work encourages students to take more responsibility for their own learning process.

Any creative process is by definition self-reflective. An artist is constantly evaluating the work—adding, editing, making decisions. Students who choose choreography as a final project must ask themselves, Does the piece meet their aesthetic standards (use of time, space, shape, and motion)? Do the movements communicate the intended information or message? Does the content of the piece adequately show an understanding of the particular subject? When all of these questions can be answered in the affirmative, then the piece is ready for presentation to the group or class. Students can then be evaluated on their use of the movement elements as well as on the ideas they express (similar to giving two grades on a paper, one for form, the other for content).

The class can play a valuable role in this assessment process by evaluating the choreographer's aesthetic choices, the content of the material, how well the movements communicate the content, and whether enough information was given through the piece. By verbalizing the information presented in a dance, the class will reveal whether or not the movements adequately communicated what the student was trying to portray.

Peer feedback during the creation of a piece lets the choreographer know if he or she is on the right track and provides a chance for the class to help develop certain material. "Having the mother and child intertwine like that showed us an important part of their relationship. How can you develop that material to show both the trust and the conflict in the relationship? What makes them break apart?"

Group criticism is not only for the benefit of the performer. It demands that the group be observant, analytical, and articulate. "I liked it," or "I didn't like it" are not very helpful comments. Students need to be specific about what they saw and how the work could be developed. When they like something, they should be encouraged to figure out what made it likable and interesting. In aesthetic terms, Was it the changes in timing? The unusual shapes? The power of group formations? The performance qualities that elicited feelings? In terms of content, Was there enough detail portraying a character or situation? How were opposing forces reflected? Was the sequence correct? Similarly, if they didn't like a section or a piece, they should try to figure out what was missing, encourage the choreographer to explore different possibilities, and learn how to phrase comments as questions rather than as "you should do this" directives. There is, after all, no single "right" way to create a dance piece.

A peer assessment process, done with a positive and supportive attitude (encouraged and, when necessary, controlled by the teacher through constructive comments and questions), can teach students a great deal about respect for diversity and about the wide range of possibilities in problem solving. The peer assessment process also provides a chance for the performers to share hidden strengths and gifts with their classmates.

An Integrated Approach
Teaching and assessment are integrally related. In order to know whether and how to progress in teaching a subject, a teacher must assess how much and how well students have understood thus far. When children participate verbally in class, teachers are gathering information about students' grasp of the material. If students are involved kinesthetically as well, a teacher can see if they are making sense of the lesson *as it progresses.*

Factor in other advantages of kinesthetic learning—muscles can sometimes transmit information to the brain that might otherwise go in one ear and out the other; and children who need concrete experiences can be engaged through kinesthetic teaching—and the great potential of the kinesthetic assessment process becomes apparent. Kinesthetic assessment creates the possibility of both ongoing and culminating evaluations that are creative, personal, and affirming to the kinesthetic learner.

NOT EVERY TEACHER WANTS TO MOVE
Using Nonmovement Resources

There are always some teachers who like to bounce around the classroom, sit on children's desks, gesture emphatically, and sit on the floor at story time. Others are more reserved with their body language and prefer to sit on chairs, write at desks, and stand at the chalkboard.

Children, however, almost universally *love* to move. To take advantage of this great spirit by transforming what could become disruptive fidgeting into constructive learning requires you to be a good director rather than a partner in motion. In other words, you don't have to do the moving. Children don't need to be shown how to move their bodies. Instead, they need permission to move. They need structure, direction, guidance, affirmation, and sincere praise, none of which requires you to get down on the floor or leap in the air. Don't feel that you cannot teach kinesthetic lessons just because you may not be comfortable doing creative movement. Your job is to learn to be a *director.*

Maintaining Control
Your goal is to release the physical energy of the children without losing control of the situation. That's not as hard as it seems. Remember that *you* are setting the limits. Be clear and firm about your spatial boundaries, and especially about behavioral boundaries. If you do not allow bumping or out-of-control physicality, it will not take over the class. Reread Chapter 3 for a discussion on control, space, and time. It will help you create a situation of freedom for the children and control

for you. Remember, children *want* to move, they want to participate in kinesthetic lessons. They do not want to sit on the side or be made to leave the room while everyone else is having fun!

Demonstrating Lessons

In order to clarify your directions, you may feel a need to show the children what you mean. Again, they can supply the movements. For instance, if you want students to contrast low-level, medium-level, and high-level shapes, ask for volunteers to demonstrate these shapes for the whole class. This will also give you a chance to point out details and nuances: "Notice how Alex is using his hands so he can balance on one leg. Alex, can you find an even more unusual place for your hands to help you balance? What other body part could you use instead of your hands?"

As you give verbal directions for a science lesson, you may have a small group demonstrate what you are saying so that you can immediately clarify any misconceptions. This provides different children with the opportunity to shine in front of the class. Some children may be embarrassed when you call on them to read out loud, but welcome the chance to set an example for the class in a kinesthetic lesson.

Using Your Own Resources

To be successful in any endeavor, you've got to "use what you got," and call upon your strengths. If moving doesn't suit you, use what does. Most teachers feel very comfortable using their voices with expression. You can communicate a great deal by varying the tempo, volume, and pitch of your words. If you whisper, the children will imitate the quietness with small, light movements. If you are loud, their movements will be bolder. If you "talk-very-quicky" they will quicken their speed. High and low sounds can accentuate high and low movements. The more texture and quality you express with your voice, the more information you give the students about how they should move.

Teachers who feel comfortable playing percussion instruments can guide children by musical accompaniment. Bells, rainsticks, triangles, tambourines, hand drums, xylophones, and maracas are some of the simpler instruments that can help children with dynamics, beginnings and endings, tempo and quality. Needless to say, teachers who are musicians can use any instrument to accompany and support movement activities. All of these resources will encourage students to gather information widely and translate from one medium to another.

DEMONSTRATING POTENTIAL AND KINETIC ENERGY

Subject
Potential and Kinetic Energy

Objectives
To allow the children to physically experience the meaning of potential
and kinetic energy

Time Allotment
30–40 minutes total

Space Requirements
A safe open space, preferably a gym

Materials and Suggested Music
Vibrant music is optional for all the activities. For part two, a mat.

Group Format
    I. Whole class
   II. Demonstrators and observers
  III. Partners
  IV. Demonstrators and observers
   V. Groups of four to five children

Lesson Plan

I. After defining the terms *potential* and *kinetic energy,* ask children to
stand with their arms at their sides, and then tell them to drop their
arms. Next have them hold their arms out parallel to the floor, and
then tell them to drop their arms. Finally have them reach their arms
straight overhead. Again tell them to drop their arms. Ask: "In which
position was the potential energy the greatest? Which motion had the
greatest kinetic energy?"

Now direct the children to swing one arm from the side (parallel
to the floor) down in front of the body and up the other side. Continue swinging from side to side. Ask: "At which point is the potential
energy the greatest? As the arm lowers, what happens to the potential
energy? At which point is the kinetic energy the highest? What happens to the kinetic energy as the arm comes up the other side? What
happens to the potential energy?"

Discuss the definitions again, now that they've been grasped physically.

II. Select four students and two helpers. Bring them onto a mat.

> One (A) lies down.
> Another (B) sits up.
> A third (C) stands.
> A fourth (D) sits on the shoulders of the two helpers.
>
> Ask each child to "fall."
> A has nowhere to go.
> B falls from sitting.
> C falls from standing, with a thud.
> D yells, "No way!"

The class observes the children and talks to them about their experiences of falling (their kinetic energy); the class determines which had the most potential energy.

III. Have children stand at a "starting line" with their feet together and a partner observing. "On your marks, get set, go!"—the children run halfway across the room as fast as they can. The observing partners mark where each child was on his or her second step.

Next, the runners stand at the starting line in a runner's starting crouch. "On your marks, get set, go!"—and again, the observing partners mark where each was on the second step.

Have the class examine the differences in the two marks and discuss why they were able to get further when beginning in the crouched position.

IV. Arrange the children in a "whip," clasping each other's wrists. The child at one end holds onto a pole or stands on an "X" on the floor, then "whips" the others around. After the fun subsides, discuss with the children which of them had the most kinetic and potential energy. Ask: "What happens to the kinetic energy as the whip is lengthened?" Try two children, then three, then five. "What happens to the kinetic energy when the speed is increased?" First go slowly around, then quickly.

V. Divide the class into groups of four to five children. Instruct the groups to create their own dances based on the themes of potential and kinetic energy using swing, fall, drop, spring, and whip as the basic movements. Encourage children to be creative in their use of timing, space, levels, floor patterns, and group formations. After the dances are rehearsed and performed, ask the class to discuss which parts of the dances showed kinetic or potential energy; which parts had the greatest and least potential and kinetic energy.

Observation

All artists are observers. They may notice sounds, colors, shapes, movements, textures, contrasts, light, patterns, or phrases—but they consciously observe. This is a skill you can pass on to your students without having to move with or for them. By describing in words how you see them moving, you will bring a wealth of information to their consciousness about shape, timing, space, motion, qualities, and meaning.

The first step is to make them aware of what they are doing. Then you can help them make choices to expand their movements by asking pointed questions: What if you vary the timing, the level, the intensity? How can you extend that into your whole body? Where should your focus be? Students can practice this skill as they take the role of the audience or the critic. As they become more observant with each other, they will also be more aware of themselves and their own choices.

Viewing Performances

In addition to observing each other, children can be exposed to movement possibilities through dance videos and live performances. When viewing videos, don't just set up the tape and watch. Prepare children for what they will see; ask them to look for specific aspects of the performance; stop the tape in the middle to highlight a particular point. Similarly, though you can't stop a live performance in the middle, many performers will agree to come back onstage after the show to answer questions from the children. Some programs actually have study guides available, with movement activities for you to do with your class prior to and following the performance to deepen the children's experience.

Watching professional performers will often inspire children to try out some of what they've observed. You can provide them with a simple structure to experiment with some of these movement ideas. You can also use a piece of the performance as the starting place for one of your own lessons: Remember when the dancers came together and went apart, came together and went apart? How is this similar to magnetic poles?

Using Gestures and Words

The most natural way to teach a kinesthetic lesson without demonstrating whole-body movements is by gesturing with your hands and arms. Gestures are a familiar part of communication, and with a little exaggeration they can express almost any movement information. Levels, spatial relationships, and timing can all be specified by gestures. Clapping the appropriate rhythms can communicate running (XXXXXXXX) versus skipping (X XX XX XX) versus walking (X X X X). Fingers and hands can give graphic information about shape and quality.

Underlying these visual and auditory cues is the power of your words. Giving students verbal directions about movement activity increases their listening skills as they translate words into movement. Absorbing information in one medium and expressing it in another deepens the process of comprehension.

Your Own Comfort

Though you may not have done this since your student teaching days, practice giving your lesson at home, or in a mirror. Say even the obvious aloud for practice. If you have access to a small group of children, try it out on them. You must be comfortable with your role as director.

Trusting your instincts as a teacher will put you in control of the situation. Start with simple, small activities. Your first kinesthetic lesson may involve only arm gestures performed while sitting at desks. When you see how engaged the children become and the results of the lesson, your confidence will grow and you'll want to do more next time.

Be attentive to the response of the children. If they are getting bored or confused, try a new approach or go on to something else. Having a fun game ready will let them release their physical energy and remember this as a positive experience. After rethinking your approach, try again.

As with anything new, kinesthetic teaching will become more comfortable the more you do it and the more you succeed. Students will not only have fun, but will actually be engaging academic concepts or subject matter. You won't have to "dance" in front of your students to channel their physical energy into kinesthetic lessons. But better not make any vows about not moving. You just may find yourself being drawn in.

LESSON PLANS

This section is designed to help you get your feet wet, to make the first five chapters more concrete, to inspire your own ideas, and to provide you with material for lessons that have all been tried in the classroom with positive results. The lesson plans that follow represent a diverse sampling of subjects and approaches. Some are useful to introduce a topic; others require some previous knowledge of the topic and are helpful in furthering a child's understanding; still others allow a child to be reflective about his or her own ideas.

The format of the presentations varies. Some provide you with the actual words to use to convey a mood or bring children through an experience, as in the lessons on molecular motion or Native Americans. Others merely lay out the structure of the lesson, as in the lessons on geometric shapes or architectural principles. Most of the lessons include questions to ask the children to help them bridge the gap between their kinesthetic experience and the subject at hand.

While many of the lessons require little or no movement from the teacher, there are some in which the teacher's involvement will be crucial to the success of the lesson, such as with the Underground Railroad. There are also situations where children will benefit most from the contributions of a guest artist. Choose the lessons that feel most comfortable for you, and allow the others to stimulate original ideas of your own.

The lesson plans on multicultural curriculum cannot adequately describe the techniques and styles of authentic dance forms in the detail necessary for you to teach them. Teachers are encouraged to seek out people native to the cultures being studied, and/or expert in their knowledge, especially professional performers. Rather than teaching specific dances, the activities described here are meant to provide pathways to understanding the values, aesthetics, or histories of diverse cultures by creating personal kinesthetic experiences. They should be presented with the acknowledgement that cultures are not monolithic. (For instance, there must be hundreds of cultural differences between the many tribes of Native Americans, and yet many of us speak of Native Americans as if they were from one culture. And while many of us may more easily distinguish between Spanish and Polish cultures, we may not necessarily differentiate between Nigerian and Kenyan peoples, or even between the various cultures within Nigeria and Kenya.) The activities included, therefore, are meant to highlight cultural features that link people within a larger framework.

Finally, you are invited to comment on your experiences using any of these lessons, or share other kinesthetic activities you have created or come across that engage your students and bring dynamic energy into the classroom. You can send your correspondence to: Susan Griss, 30 Old Whitfield Road, Accord, NY 12404.

Kinesthetic language is one of the oldest and most primal forms of communication. It has played a significant role in the ritual life of ancient people. Adding our contributions to the development of kinesthetic teaching is part of a long and great tradition.

LANGUAGE ARTS
LESSON PLANS

DRILLING GRAMMAR

Objectives
To provide an opportunity for children to drill lessons in grammar; to engage children in grammatical exercises; to make grammar lessons physical so that they can be recalled more easily

Time Allotment
10 minutes each

Space Requirements
The classroom is fine; open space is best

Materials and Suggested Music
Cards with specific words; a drum; or friendly background music

Group Format
The whole class working together

Lesson Plan

I. Hold up a card with a printed word. Instruct the children to make a long shape if the word has a long vowel sound, or a short shape if the word has a short vowel sound: i.e., hug, huge, bit, bite, beetle, battle, etc.

II. Hold up a card with a printed word. Instruct the children to make a still shape if the word is a noun, move without traveling if the word is an adjective, and travel if the word is a verb.

III. Hold up a card with two printed words. Instruct the children to make the shape of the word that comes first in the dictionary: ball or candle? triangle or square? table or tall? arrow or apple?

IV. Hold up a card with a printed word. Instruct the children to make the shape of or move the antonym of the word: up, fast, small, wide, crooked, happy, closed.

PUNCTUATION

Objectives
To teach children proper use of punctuation marks; to provide a kinesthetic and enjoyable way for children to drill punctuation

Time Allotment
15–30 minutes

Space Requirements
Almost anywhere

Materials and Suggested Music
A chalkboard or large pad on which to write sentences for the entire class to see

Group Format
The whole class working together

Lesson Plan

With the whole class, express punctuation marks physically by creating simple whole body movements (i.e., stretching tall for a capital letter, squatting for a period, sustained and sudden movements to pause and separate for a comma, two hands by the mouth like you are calling someone for opening quotation marks, and two hands by the ears like you are listening for closing quotation marks). In small groups, one at a time, or the whole class together, the children then *walk* (pantomime) an unpunctuated sentence which they read aloud from the chalkboard, adding the appropriate punctuation movements as they go.

(A teacher once commented that after this lesson, students who had rarely used punctuation in their writing were not only using it consistently, but using it correctly.)

CREATIVE WRITING

Objectives
    I. To help children experience and articulate the emotional state of a character
    II. To help children articulate physical details of a character

Time Allotment
Approximately 30 minutes total

Space Requirements
Space for everyone to move but not necessarily one big open space

Materials and Suggested Music
    I. Drum; groups of cards with an emotion written on each one
    II. Short descriptive writing by the students describing a character

Group Format
    I. The whole class working together
    II. Working individually

Lesson Plan

I. Ask the students to name as many feelings as they can think of, to generate thinking about a variety of emotions. Then, using examples from the list, play the freeze game:

When you bang the drum once and stop, students freeze in a position that expresses the emotion you have called out.

When you signal with the drum again, students move the feelings of that pose or emotion.

Encourage the students to pay particular attention to the shape of their poses (open or closed, high or low, shoulders raised or lowered, etc.); their muscle tension (tight or released); their focus (inward or outward); other movement qualities (jerky or smooth, fast or slow).

Students can also play a game in groups of about eight. Put a stack of "emotion" cards in the middle of the circle, face down. A student picks the top card and acts out or "moves" the emotion. The other students guess the word on the card.

II. Ask the students to write a description of a character in a particular mood (a lonely child, an angry girl, a sad man). Then have the children improvise movements that express what the person is feeling. Try to differentiate between what the character is *doing* (i.e., screaming, throwing a shoe) and what the character is *feeling* (i.e., explosive, furious, betrayed). You might ask them to exaggerate their movements, and guide them with the following questions.

Which expresses the feeling more truly:

inward or outward focus?
tight or free muscles?
sudden and jerky or continuous and smooth movements?
moving fast or slow or a combination?
moving with small or large movements?
taking up a lot of space or a little space?
moving with clear direction or every which way?

After students explore the physicality of the emotion or mood, have them rewrite the description using details of what they just experienced in terms of feelings as well as physical movements.

POETRY

This lesson plan can be applied to Multicultural Curriculum as "Poetry from Diverse Cultures."

Objectives
To help children comprehend poetry; to enhance children's enjoyment of poetry; to help children understand metaphor

Time Allotment
Varies

Space Requirements
Enough open space to move freely

Materials and Suggested Music
Pass It On: African-American Poetry for Children, by Wade Hudson;
The Random House Book of Poetry for Children, edited by Jack Prelutsky; *Dancing Teepees,* edited by Virginia Driving Hawk Sneve; *Be My Friend,* by Edith Segal; *A Child's Garden of Verses,* by Robert Louis Stevenson; *I dream of peace,* produced by UNICEF. Can be done to silence or any music that reflects a particular poem and/or its ethnicity.

Group Format
Everyone together, or five to eight children at a time while the rest of the class is the audience

Lesson Plan

Children improvise the *feelings* of a poem, focusing on both the physical and emotional responses that it evokes. Studying the poem, "When I Was Lost," by Dorothy Aldis (Prelutsky 1983, 120), a class of hearing-impaired children who had no previous exposure to poetry did not understand Aldis' metaphor, "My stomach was a stone" until they were "moving" the poem.

Children can also dance the story of a poem to have a more personal experience with it. For instance, in Carl Sandburg's famous poem "Fog," the fog "comes on little cat feet" (Prelutsky 1983, 96). Children can climb into this poem and its metaphors by dancing as both the cat and the fog.

In the following poem by Edith Segal (1952, 16), children can experience the difference between being caged (trapped inside a circle) and being free (allowed to "spread their wings" and fly all over the room).

IF I WERE A BIRD

If I were a bird,
I wouldn't like to be
In a little cage
Where I couldn't be free.

I'd like to spread
My wings and fly
Over the tree-tops
And into the sky.

First and second graders dancing to the poem, "If I Were a Bird"

I'd visit my friends
Who live very far
Then I'd fly up high
And sit on a star.

If a poem is short enough, let the children listen to the complete poem before they begin to move. Then you can either read the poem again as they improvise, pausing to give them time to explore the images through movement, or you can complete your reading and then let them dance the feeling of the whole poem, or of one particularly strong image.

Improvising movement to poetry from diverse cultures can help children gain insights into the aesthetics and value systems of those cultures. For instance, in "We Chased Butterflies," by Plenty-Coups Crow, a child's "first lesson" is to chase butterflies "to give us endurance" and ask the insects for the gifts of "grace and swiftness" (Sneve 1989, 19). In Langston Hughes' famous lyrical poem, "The Dream Keeper," "heart melodies" and "a blue cloud-cloth" are contrasted with the "too rough fingers of the world" (Wade 1993, 26). These images, drawn from poems published specifically for children, have deep roots in their respective cultures.

Props, such as silk scarves, long fabrics, hoops, elastic, etc., may be added to the improvisations. Or you may wish to use a shadow screen made of white fabric held up by two poles. Light the screen from behind with an overhead projector or a slide projector with a white or colored transparency inserted. To introduce children to the shadow screen they can improvise to some verses from the famous poem by Robert Louis Stevenson (1929, 38):

My Shadow

I have a little shadow that goes in and out with me,
And what can be the use of him is more than I can see.
He is very, very like me from the heels up to the head;
And I see him jump before me, when I jump into my bed.

The funniest thing about him is the way he likes to grow—
Not at all like proper children, which is always very slow;
For he sometimes shoots up taller like an india-rubber ball,
And sometimes gets so little that there's none of him at all.

For children in the upper elementary grades, poetry can offer a way to grapple with some of the world's overwhelming problems. *I dream of peace* (UNICEF 1993) contains images of war in a collection of poetry and drawings by children of former Yugoslavia. Creating group dances based on the stories and feelings of the poems allows children a safe way to imagine and explore troubling aspects of the larger world.

Children should begin with whatever stands out from the poem, rather than with the first line. If a group is having difficulty finding movements, they may begin by creating a frozen tableau that depicts the feeling or theme of a poem, or a set of tableaux that captures a variety of images. Bringing these still poses to life can inspire movements. Improvising the feelings that motivate the shapes will deepen the understanding of the poem.

Using metaphors and vividly descriptive language, the poems in this collection range from devastating to hopeful and visionary:

War . . . is a deadly bird that destroys our homes, and deprives us of our childhood.

—Maida, 12, from Skopje (39)

If I were President . . .
the guns would blossom with flowers.

—Roberto, 10, from Pula (72)

Group choreographies can be woven together to create a full dance piece performed to this poetry.

SOCIAL STUDIES
LESSON PLANS

COLONIAL PERIOD

Objectives
To view the social order of the Colonial period through one of its dance forms

Time Allotment
25 minutes

Space Requirements
Enough space for your group to do a couples dance in long lines

Materials and Suggested Music
    I. Drum
    II. Colonial dance music entitled "Galopede" or any colonial dance music in three parts

You may wish to obtain *Chimes of Dunkirk Great Dances for Children* that can be ordered with a music cassette from:

New England Dancing Masters
6 Willow Street
Brattleboro, Vermont 05301

You can also find this and other dances in a collection called *Colonial Social Dancing for Children* by Charles Hendrickson, which can be ordered from:

Hendrickson
PO Box 766
Sandy Hook, Connecticut 06482

Group Format
The whole class together

Lesson Plan

I. First, ask the children to walk around the space however they want to for approximately thirty seconds. Don't give them specific instructions as to what floor pattern, what speed, what direction, etc. Bang the drum to signal them to stop.

Next, ask them to line up in two lines facing each other about six feet apart, girls on one side, boys on the other. When you direct them with the drum, they walk four steps toward each other, then four steps back, and then eight steps across so that they change places with the person in the opposite line, passing right shoulders. Repeat the whole sequence so they are back in their original places.

Which felt more organized? Chaotic? Restricted? In Colonial times, the immigrants left an ordered European society and arrived in a wilderness full of unknowns. Bringing dance forms from their homeland provided some comfort. Maintaining these formal dance structures helped them cope with the confusion and chaos of building a new society and government in a new land.

II. This simple line dance called Galopede was danced by George Washington. It is danced with a slight air of jest to make fun of the artistocracy back in Europe.

The class forms sets of two lines with partners facing each other, approximately six feet apart (no more than six couples per set). The musicians and the prompter (caller) should be at one end of the line called the *head* of the line. When dancers move toward the *head* of the line they are moving *up*. Toward the other end is *down*. The prompter calls the instructions *before the downbeat* of each phrase. This dance has three parts.

Part I

PROMPTER'S CALL	COUNTS	DIRECTIONS
Forward and back	1–4	Walk 3 steps toward your partner (R,L,R) and slap both hands with your partner's hands.
	5–8	Walk 3 steps backward to place (L,R,L) and hold.
Cross over	9–16	Walk 8 steps across to exchange places with your partner, passing right shoulders with your partner on the way.
	1–16	Repeat the first 16 counts to return to your original place.

Part II

Right hand turn	1–8	Doing 8 walking steps: meet your partner in the middle and do one full elegant turn clockwise holding each other's right hand pinkies aloft, ending back in your original places.
Left hand turn	9–16	Repeat counts 1–8 turning counterclockwise holding left hand pinkies aloft. Everyone ends back in their original places.

Part III

Head couple down the center, everybody clap	1–16	The head couple takes hands and chassés or does a two-hand turn *down* the middle of the two lines and takes their places at the end. The rest of the group moves one place *up* toward the head of the set while clapping 8 sets of three claps (1, and, 2; 3, and, 4; 5, and, 6; and so on, to 16). There is now a new head couple.

After every couple has had a chance to be at the head, you may add this special ending to the dance: When the head couple is halfway down the middle doing their chassé step, the next head couple begins to chassé down the line. When this couple is halfway down, the next couple begins to chassé down, and so on, creating a wave. Everyone else keeps up the clapping rhythm of Part III, moving up the line until it is their turn to chassé down the middle.

THE U. S. CONSTITUTION

Objectives
    I. To demonstrate the growth of enfranchisement and the living quality of the Constitution
   II. To help children understand the concept of checks and balances
  III. To demonstrate the mechanics of government as set up by the Constitution

Time Allotment
Approximately 30 minutes each

Space Requirements
    I. The classroom is adequate
   II. Requires open space
  III. Can be done in a classroom, but open space is preferable

Materials and Suggested Music
   II. Music by Philip Glass or Steve Reich is helpful (ongoing flowing, driving music)
  III. Any music can be chosen

Group Format
    I. Whole class working together
   II. In groups of three
  III. Whole class working together

Lesson Plan

I. Ask the children to imagine that they are adults. "Stand up if you are guaranteed the right to vote in United States elections." While they continue to stand, take them back through history to the time of the writing of the Constitution. "If you are female, sit down, women did not have the right to vote. If you are Native American or African American sit down, Native Americans and African Americans were not entitled to vote. Those of you who are still standing, if you do not

**Feeling the three-way pull of checks and
balances described in the U. S. Constitution**

own your home, sit down. Only property holding men were allowed to vote." Observe the difference in the number of children standing at the beginning and end of this exercise. Then reverse the order, and discuss the XVth and XIXth amendments to the Constitution, how states guaranteed more and more people the right to vote over the years, and the struggles involved to change the laws.

II. Checks and balances between the Congress, Presidency, and the Legislature, are complex and create many challenges. Students can recreate the intricate balance of three distinct forces always connected to each other, trying to maintain a group balance. In groups of three, have the children connect body parts to the two others in the group so that each is able to lean away while staying attached, and not fall down. Once they are able to find their balance (while leaning off balance), have them try constantly changing positions, always remaining connected to their two partners, always leaning off balance as an individual, yet staying balanced as a group. The most challenging part is to keep this going while trying to travel across the floor or "leading the nation forward."

III. Set out the rules of the Constitution as they apply to governing. The President is the choreographer. The President is chosen by a majority of the class and serves for four years with the chance for another term. (If you are ambitious, you can set up an "electoral college" system.) The choreographer can choreograph for four (or whatever you decide) minutes, and if reelected can do another four minutes. A group of students is appointed by the President (with the approval of the rest of the class) to be the Supreme Court. This group will make decisions on any conflicts between the class and the President. The rest of the class makes a few rules governing the dance, for example:

- The dance will have six performers.
- There will be an equal number of girl and boy performers.
- The dance will be no longer than five minutes in length.
- Taped music will be used.
- The dance format will be A B A.

In addition there will be a short Bill of Rights, agreed to by the whole class. This will guarantee that:

- No one is forced to perform.
- No one is forced to do a movement they feel uncomfortable doing. (This may need interpretation by the Supreme Court!)
- No one is asked to do something dangerous.
- No one may intentionally physically hurt or embarrass anyone else.

You may add whatever else is appropriate.

This can be an ongoing project. Rules can be changed according to correct procedure. An evaluation of the difficulties, strengths, and protections of this method will be an important part of the lesson. Also discuss the ways in which creating a dance is *not* like running a nation.

SLAVE SHIPS

Objectives
To help children comprehend the inhumanity of the slave ships

Time Allotment
Approximately 30 minutes

Space Requirements
Large open space

Materials and Suggested Music
African drumming dance music such as by Olatunji; diagram showing
how people were packed in a slave ship

Group Format
The whole class together

Lesson Plan

This was inspired by a lesson taught by Livia Vanaver from *Dance: A
Social Study*, a dance curriculum produced by ArtsConnection, NYC.

Teach children an African dance with bright, energetic, open
movements. (This is a perfect time to bring in a guest artist.) While
they are in the middle of dancing it, stop the class abruptly. In a harsh
manner, arrange the children according to the actual diagrams of the
slave ships. They will lay *very* close to each other, each having only 16"
across and $2\frac{1}{2}'$ of vertical space. Don't let them move or talk. Don't
tell them why. Tell them they must remain silent in these positions for
five minutes. Threaten severe consequences for breaking the rules.

At the end of five minutes (usually harder for the teacher than
the kids), break the spell. Become yourself again, the teacher that they
know and feel safe with. Ask them if they know what just happened.
Discuss the details of being kidnapped and transported across the
ocean on a slave ship. Draw comparisons between the uncomfortable
experience they just had for five minutes and the five weeks of terror
and physical oppression of the historical reality.

U. S. LABOR HISTORY

Objectives
To help children understand the labor struggles of the early 1900s:
I. Crowded sweatshops; the motivations for unionizing, II. The hard-
ships of striking, and III. The rhythm of organizing

Time Allotment
I and II.   20 minutes each
III.   Two 45-minute sessions plus time for showing pieces

Space Requirements
Large open space

Materials and Suggested Music
I. Philip Glass' *Music for Changing Parts* or any driving, mechanical music; two or three pieces of cloth, each about five yards long and approximately 60" wide; a whistle

II. A rendition of "Bread and Roses" or any labor songs from that time period

III. Any music with a strong downbeat, emphasized by a live drum

Group Format
I and II.   The whole class works together

III.   The class is divided into groups of four to six students

Lesson Plan

I. After describing the physical conditions of New York City sweatshops, have the class stand around the edges of the three cloths, holding the fabric waist high, as if they were large work tables. Doing a simple rocking movement back and forth and small hand movements "working" the cloth, the children imitate the motions of sewing garments on old sewing machines. While they work, a few students walk around them acting as the inside contractors, demanding that they work faster, that they stop talking, yelling at them for breaking a needle, etc. The "dancers"—workers—are not allowed to talk back. They keep working without a break, imagining the heat (wiping sweat from a brow), the long hours, and dim light, etc. Remind them that in many factories the doors were locked so they couldn't even go to the bathroom without permission. Even fire doors were locked. As the speed increases, the movement is exaggerated into a chaos of motion and fabric so that the inside contractors blow a whistle, and the work is halted . . . temporarily. Discuss the similarities and differences between factories of today and those of the early 1900s, and the process of change.

II. Set up a picket line—walking around in a shallow circle—with most of the class. The rest of the class becomes police officers and thugs. As the picketers walk around in the "wintry cold street of New York City," the thugs tease and taunt them, trying to get them out of line without having actual physical contact. (Explain that the real thugs did have physical contact with the strikers, including breaking ribs, spitting, etc.) The strikers try to ignore the thugs. Whenever there appears to be trouble, have two police officers arrest the striker taking him or her off to a corner to be "arraigned." After a few moments the striker can rejoin the picket line getting out "on bail." At a point of chaos, signal for a *freeze* using a drum or whistle. Discuss the challenges of organizing labor and the role of the labor unions.

III. (This is a challenging activity that takes serious rehearsal, but is very rewarding and fun to watch.)

The process of organizing a union starts with a minority and grows to a majority. There are moments of connection and clarity along the way, mixed with confusion and disorder, culminating in a sense of unity and strength. The accumulation in a fuguelike dance form parallels this process in miniature. In the following example, each of four parts may be performed by one or two people.

Each part goes through the pattern 1; 1, 2; 1, 2, 3; 1, 2, 3, 4; 1, 2, 3, 4, 5.

Every number has a corresponding movement lasting one measure. The movements should be choreographed by the children, and reflect an aspect of organizing, i.e., reaching out to others, feeling strong and committed, being defiant, feeling nervous, feeling empowered. Movement number 1 should have a strong downbeat including a sound, like a clap or a stamp, that will help keep the rhythm. Drumming the downbeat for each measure will help the dancers stay on the beat.

The arrow between each set of numbers indicates that the performer runs to a new position. The children should set their places so

A – RUNS AFTER EACH PHRASE
B – NEVER RUNS AFTER 5
C – RUNS AFTER EACH PHRASE
D – DOES NOT RUN AFTER FIRST 5, RUNS AFTER SECOND 5
↑ = RUN
! = HOLD POSITION

Accumulation chart

that they know where to run after each phrase. The "!" in the last measure indicates the dancers hold their final shape.

Part A begins the dance. Part B enters on the third measure. Part C enters on the sixth measure, and Part D on the seventh. B, C, and D enter running for a full measure to their places.

If you highlight the accumulation chart (on p. 81) in yellow wherever two parts have the same numbers (i.e., parts A and B each have an arrow, 1 and 2 for measures 5–7; B and D each have arrow, 1, 2, 3 for measures 12–15; A, C, and D have 1, 2, 3, 4, 5 for measures 27–31) you will find longer and longer phrases of unison movements within the dance, until it ends with all of the dancers in unison dancing 1, 2, 3, 4, 5 for measures 33–37.

The notes under the chart are tips for each part.

Have patience . . . good luck!!

SCIENCE
LESSON PLANS

SOIL EROSION/PREVENTION

Objectives
To demonstrate the importance of plants in preventing soil erosion

Time Allotment
10 minutes

Space Requirements
An open space at least 10×15 feet

Materials and Suggested Music
Silence or any instrumental music

Group Format
The whole class works together

Lesson Plan

Divide the class into two groups. One group represents the soil and
each child gets into the shape of a grain of soil (curled up tight like a
ball). Ask the soil to roll away carried by wind and water, while the rest
of the class observes. Next ask the soil to return to their original
places, and this time arrange the rest of the class throughout the space
like plants (or trees) growing up here and there wherever there is soil.

Plants, soil, and the wind showing the prevention of soil erosion

The plants should stand with feet placed about two feet apart so they can be firmly "planted." Again ask the soil to roll away carried by water and wind, and watch them roll right into the plants, stopped from continuing their journey. Let them discuss how the plants prevented the soil from eroding, and explain the significance of plants and trees in preventing erosion in the natural world.

ANIMALS

Objectives
To heighten awareness of differences and similarities in animal behavior based on physical properties

Time Allotment
15 minutes

Space Requirements
Open space, not necessarily large

Drum; any instrumental background music

Group Format
The entire class working together, or taking turns in smaller groups with the rest of the class observing

Lesson Plan

This activity is in the format of the freeze game (see Chapter 3) where children act out your directions. When the drum bangs, they freeze in an appropriate shape and wait for the next direction. The following suggestions will guide you:

> Every animal has to eat. How would you eat if you were a:
> horse, chicken, lizard, monkey, mosquito, fish, squirrel, elephant?
>
> How would you travel if you were a:
> rabbit, snake, cheetah, tortoise, eagle, crab, gorilla, penguin, fish, spider, human, slug?
>
> How would you scratch your back if you were a:
> dog, bird, lion, giraffe, chimp?
>
> How and where would you sleep if you were a:
> fox, cow, snake, bird, human, mole, fish?
>
> How would you clean yourself if you were a:
> lion, chimp, bird, elephant, dog, human?
>
> How would you defend yourself if you were a:
> skunk, tiger, turtle, gorilla, dog, snake, bee, prairie dog, antelope, starfish?

SIMPLE MACHINES: THE LEVER AND THE INCLINED PLANE

Objectives
To allow children to discover principles of I. The lever and II. The inclined plane through their bodies.

Time Allotment
20–30 minutes total

Space Requirements
  I. Can be done in a classroom
  II. Needs a clear space of about 20 × 10 feet

Materials and Suggested Music
  I. A ball
  II. A pile of mats about two and a half feet high for children to run onto, plus enough to make stepping stones up to the top

Group Format
  I. The class will observe a demonstrator
  II. The class will work as a group

Lesson Plan

I. *The Lever*

Ask the class which lever will have more force, one with a shorter arm or a longer one. Then place a child in front of the room holding a small ball. Using only the hand from the wrist to the fingers, ask the child to throw the ball. Mark where the ball landed. Explain that in this third class lever (the fulcrum is at one end and the resistence at the other), the wrist is the fulcrum, the ball the resistance, and the hand is the "arm" of the lever. When the ball is retrieved and returned, ask the child to extend the arm of the lever all the way to the elbow, and to throw the ball using only the hand and lower arm. Again mark where the ball landed. Finally, ask the child to extend the arm all the way to the shoulder, and to throw the ball using the hand, lower, and upper arm. Discuss which throw had the most force and which had the longest arm. Make the connections to other levers.

II. *The Inclined Plane*

Stack the mats so that they resemble stairs leading up to a platform of mats approximately two and a half feet high (adjust the height depending on the general height of students in your class). One at a time have the children run up the mats to the top and then jump off. Ask the children to observe the amount of effort that was needed to reach the top. Then remove the stepping stone mats, leaving only the platform. When the children have rested, ask them again to run up the mats and then jump off. Ask them to observe the amount of effort needed to reach the top this time, and to compare the difference. Explain that the stairs are an inclined plane reducing the amount of effort needed to produce the work of arriving on top.

WATER MOLECULES

Objectives

I. To demonstrate the effect of changing temperature on water molecules; to help children become aware that water is the only known natural substance that can be in the form of liquid, solid, or gas

II. To demonstrate the molecular structure of water as liquid, solid, and vapor

Time Allotment
15 minutes

Space Requirements
Indoor or outdoor open space

Materials and Suggested Music
A drum

Group Format
The whole class will work as one group

Lesson Plan

I. Discuss with the children what percentage of the surface of the earth is water, and what percentage of a human body is made of water. Then ask the children to stand in a circle and move their bodies fluidly like water while you play the drum. While the children are moving (nonlocomotor) start slowing down the drum and ask what happens to water when it gets colder, and colder, and colder. Bang the drum once more and stop (the children's signal to freeze). "It turns to ice," they will say. Next say, "When I bang the drum once more, turn into an ice sculpture [bang]. Now make an ice sculpture on a different level [bang]; and another level [bang]."

"Let's warm the ice. What will happen?" As you play the drum a little faster, the ice will melt into water molecules again. Keep playing the drum faster and faster telling them it's getting hotter and hotter. Ask, "What do you think will happen to the water?" Briefly discuss evaporation as the children move about with more motion (they can add locomotion) to the faster drum beat. Now you can cool them down again by slowing down the tempo and they will become water again, ice again, water, vapor, water, and finally end in ice sculptures, which can melt into puddles onto the floor.

II. (For older children.) After discussing the chemical composition of H_2O, divide the class into groups of three. Each group will decide who will be the oxygen atom and who will be the hydrogen atoms. Each oxygen atom will extend both arms out diagonally to the sides, forming an angle of approximately 105 degrees. The hydrogen atoms will face the oxygen atom and clasp the oxygen's extended hand with *one* of their own hands. (A hydrogen's right hand will grasp the oxygen's right hand; the other hydrogen's left hand will grasp the oxygen's left hand.) These are now water molecules, and they can move around the room as long as each trio stays connected to itself. As the drum speeds up, the children will move faster using more space, but must stay in their formations of three. This is the water vapor stage.

Slowing down the drum, the children will become liquid once again. Now ask each hydrogen atom to attach itself to a second oxygen atom—*without letting go of the first*—by standing *behind* the new oxygen atom and placing their free hand on the back shoulder of the new oxygen. *No oxygen atom can have more than three hydrogen atoms attached to itself,* but many water molecules may be strung together in this formation. Please note: Not all hydrogen atoms will find a free oxygen shoulder. You will end up with several clumps of attached molecules. These are ice crystals! And as you can imagine, they don't move around very much.

By changing the tempo of the drum, and calling out the appropriate form (liquid, solid, or gas), allow the children to experience the different structural states of water.

MOLECULAR MOTION

Objectives
To give the students an awareness of the molecular motion (energy) that surrounds them in all matter

Time Allotment
15 minutes

Space Requirements
Indoor or outdoor open space

Materials and Suggested Music
Six or eight hand-sized stones; a drum

Group Format
The whole class will work as one group

Lesson Plan

Sitting in a circle on the floor, pass out the stones and ask children to study them carefully, paying special attention to the tiny particles pressed together in such density as to make up the stone. As children feel their shape and weight, they are passed around until everyone has held at least one stone. Have the children place them in the center of the circle and everyone notice their stillness as they lie motionless.

Recapturing the density and stillness of a stone

Now the class will try to recapture the density and stillness of the stones in their own bodies, the whole class becoming one rock: The teacher stands with the stones in the center of the circle, and the children spread out fifteen or twenty feet away on all sides. As the teacher taps the drum lightly, the children *slowly* advance toward the teacher. As soon as the drum hits a loud bang and stops, the children freeze wherever they are. Continue this process until the children are grouped around the teacher, close but not packed, all arms down by their sides. When the group is as close as they will get, bang the drum once more and ask the children to stop fidgeting, blinking, etc. Then bang the drum once more and ask them to hold their breaths—to become "still as stones." Count to three silently and release the students to sit in their circle again. Give them a moment to share with a friend.

"How many of you felt the density and stillness of the stones? How many of you were able to be completely still? It's true that if someone were to walk by, they'd think we were still as a statue, but how many of you were able to make your heart stop beating? And what about your blood, wasn't it flowing throughout your body even as we held our breaths? Even your brain was firing chemicals to the nerves saying *Don't move! Don't move!* So while we were standing still as stones, there was really all kinds of motion happening inside where we could not see it.

"The stones too are filled with motion called energy. They are actually made up of molecules that have electrons spinning around so small and so fast that we cannot see them. Everything that we can see and touch is made of molecules and spinning electrons. So everything is motion: the chairs, the floor, your skin, the clothes you wear. You just can't see it."

NEWTON'S LAWS

Objectives
To allow children to discover the principles of force and motion in a playground

Time Allotment
45 minutes to an hour

Space Requirements
A playground

Materials and Suggested Music
I. A slide
II. Baseball bats, balls of three different weights (small and light, medium, larger and heavier); seesaw
III. Swing, heavy rock, balloon

Group Format

With supervision, the class can divide into three groups, each experiencing one of Newton's Laws. The groups can then change, so that everyone has a turn at each. Group discussions can take place in each of the three groups before bringing everyone together to share their discoveries.

Lesson Plan

I. Newton's First Law: *Inertia*

Run with speed for a distance of 50 feet. Rest.

Run with speed for a distance of 50 feet stopping and starting 10 times along the way. Rest.

Run with speed for a distance of 50 feet changing direction sharply every 10 feet. Rest.

At which moments did you feel you had to exert more effort? Which run was the easiest? Which took the most effort?

Holding right wrists, swing a partner round and round and then let go. What happens? Swing your partner round and round again and then try to stop suddenly. What happens?

Sit on top of a slide. What has to happen before you slide down? What happens when you reach the bottom of the slide? What do you think would happen if the slide did not level off at the bottom?

II. Newton's Second Law: $F = m \times a$

Use a lot of force to hit a baseball with a bat.
Use very little force to hit the same baseball with the same bat.
Which time did the ball travel faster?

Hit a small light ball with a baseball bat.
Hit a larger heavier ball with the same amount of force.
Which ball traveled faster?

Try to hit the light ball and the heavier ball the same distance. Which took the greater force?

Balancing with a friend on a seesaw, how many times can you go up and down in 30 seconds? Add another person to each side of the seesaw, but only the original two can put their feet on the ground. Using the *same* amount of force, how long does it take for you to go up and down that same number of times? If you were to do it in the same 30 seconds, would you have to push harder?

III. Newton's Third Law: *For every force (action) there is an equal and opposite force (reaction).*

Can you jump in the air without first pushing down into the floor?

Sit quietly suspended on a swing with a large rock in your lap. Throw the rock in front of you (making sure no one is there!) and see what happens to you and the swing.

Blow up a balloon and then release the air. What happens to the balloon as the air escapes? What is the relationship between the swing and the balloon?

MATH
LESSON PLANS

NUMBERS/AMOUNTS

Objectives
To help children grasp the concrete value of different number amounts

Time Allotment
10–15 minutes each

Space Requirements
Open space is best but not required

Materials and Suggested Music
For the second part, a drum and lively music with a strong, steady beat

Group Format
The whole class working together

Lesson Plan

I.

Hop on one foot once.

Jump on two feet twice.

Now do one hop, two jumps.

Let's add tapping our heads with both hands together three times.

How many body parts are we using: two hands and one head. (2 + 1 = 3)

Let's do one hop, two jumps, and three taps.

Can you jump like a frog landing on two hands and two feet?

Let's do four frog jumps. (Two hands and two feet equal four.)

Now: One hop, two jumps, three taps, four frog jumps.

Zap your fingers (on one hand) like you're doing a magic spell. How many fingers are on one hand? Let's zap five times.

Now: One hop, two jumps, three taps, four frog jumps, and five zaps.

II. In the format of the freeze game (move while the music or drum is playing and then stop still as a statue when the music stops or the drum bangs loudly and then stops):

Freeze in a shape with three limbs touching the floor.

Freeze in a shape with two different limbs in the air.

Freeze in a shape with seven fingers up.

Freeze in a shape with four body parts pointing up to the ceiling.

Freeze in a shape with only one body part touching the floor.

Freeze in a shape with three body parts pointing in different directions.

Connected to a partner, freeze in a shape with five body parts touching the floor.

You can continue making up your own. The children can also do shapes while the rest of the class says how many body parts are pointing in different directions.

PATTERNS

Objectives
    I. To allow the children to experience a variety of patterns kinesthetically; to help the children understand the concept of a pattern
    II. To allow children to create a pattern kinesthetically

Time Allotment
Two 45-minute sessions

Space Requirements
Room to move individually

Materials and Suggested Music
    I. Can be done in silence or with music with a strong beat and a clear downbeat
    II. Music with a strong beat and a clear downbeat

Group Format
    I. The whole group together
    II. Individually or in small groups

Lesson Plan

I. Create three simple gestures (A,B,C) such as tapping head, slapping thighs, snapping fingers, clapping hands, rolling shoulders, etc. Perform them sequentially three times and then stop after the first gesture of the fourth sequence: A,B,C,A,B,C,A,B,C,A. Ask the children, "What comes next?" And then, "How did you know?" Now ask them if they can perform the sequence, or unit, one time that keeps repeating in the pattern (A,B,C).

    Try a different set of gestures (X,Y,Z), and this time add a fourth gesture during the fourth sequence, and then return to the regular sequence: X,Y,Z,X,Y,Z,X,Y,Z,X,A,Y,Z,X,Y,Z. "What didn't belong? How did you know?" Again ask if they can perform the unit that keeps repeating in the pattern (X,Y,Z).

    Have the children make up a few patterns by each contributing a gesture. Keep each pattern to three gestures.

    Now try some different patterns:

A,B,B, A,B,B, A,B,B . . .

A,B, A,C, A,D, A,E . . .

A,B,B,A, A,B,B,A . . . (This one is tricky because it looks like A,A,B,B once it gets started. The children have to be observant to notice you only do A once the first time and therefore the pattern that repeats is A,B,B,A in that specific order.)

A, A,B, A,B,C, A,B,C,D . . . (This is called an *accumulation*.)

II. Ask the children, individually or in small groups, to make up their own pattern, or choose one from your list, and create whole body movements for each letter. Then they can notate the pattern they chose by creating symbols for each movement and using different colors for each symbol. The children then perform the pattern for the class, and the class has to identify the letter pattern.

GEOMETRIC SHAPES

Objectives
To help children become familiar with geometric shapes

Time Allotment
15–20 minutes each

Space Requirements
Large open space is preferred, but can be done in a smaller area

Materials and Suggested Music
I and II. Lively or classical music
III. Elastic strips about twelve feet long tied or sewn into circles

Group Format
Whole group working together

Lesson Plan

I. In the format of the freeze game, have children create shapes using their whole bodies, parts of their bodies (legs or arms or fingers, etc.) or with a partner: circle, square, rectangle, triangle, trapezoid, parallelogram, etc. Children can also construct these shapes using bodies as building blocks lying on the ground or standing.

II. With children in a single line behind you, lead them into an open space walking in the floor pattern of a particular geometric shape and let them guess the shape. With children as leaders, have them skip, slide, gallop, run, jump, etc., different floor patterns. With children grouped in four corners of the space, call out a name, a movement, and a shape: "Jennifer, skip in a diamond shape," or "Joshua, hop in the shape of a parallelogram."

III. Using strips of elastic tied into individual circles, let the children climb inside and use their bodies to stretch the elastic into spe-

Using bodies and elastic to create geometric shapes

cific geometric shapes. The bottom two corners can be held by their feet and the top two corners by their hands as a simple way to begin. This is especially clear for understanding shapes like trapezoids (feet further apart than hands), rectangles (hands directly over feet), and parallelograms (hands diagonally over from feet, but equidistant). Children can also work in small groups, each group using one elastic.

FRACTIONS

Objectives
To create a structure for students to kinesthetically experience fractions through rhythm; to help students add mixed fractions that equal one whole

Time Allotment
30–45 minutes

Space Requirements
Room to move, preferably an open space

Materials and Suggested Music
Friendly music with a steady beat and a strong downbeat; a drum

Group Format

    I. Working as a whole group

    II. Working individually or in small groups

Lesson Plan

I. Warm up the class clapping to the music (loud on the first beat of each phrase, soft on other beats): 8, 4, 4, 2, 2, 2, 2, 1, 1, 1, 1, 1, 1, 1, 1. Do the same thing walking on each beat and change direction as you clap on every first beat. Discuss how many phrases of four make up a phrase of eight. Each phrase is half of the whole. You need four phrases of two, and each is one quarter of the whole.

II. Take eight running steps, clapping eight times in rhythm. Notate the eight runs: *XXXXXXXX.* Ask: "How many skips can I do during the same eight claps?" Have the class clap the rhythm while you (or a student) skip. (Four skips) Children create a notation symbol for the skips and notate.

Children clap eight more times as you (or a student) do body swings with a jump (or any movement that takes four counts). "How many swings did I do during the same eight claps?" (Two swings) Children create a notation symbol for the swings and notate.

Children clap eight more times as you (or a student) run in a circle, ending with a pivot turn (or any movement that takes eight counts). "How many times did I run in a circle during the same eight claps?" (One time) Children create a notation symbol for the circle and notate.

Make a chart. Each section will represent eight claps. Begin with two running steps. Have a child notate the two runs. "What shall I do next?" (One skip?) Another child notates the skip. "How many claps have we used up? [Four] I'll clap, you do two runs and one skip. What else can we do to fill out the remaining four claps?"

Make up more sections (which are actually musical measures) on the chart and have the children first notate and then do the movements to the beat of a drum.

Have the children, individually or in small groups, make up their own charts (scores) using their own movements and their own symbols. Each will have four different movements: an eight-count movement, a four-count movement, a two-count movement, and a single-count movement. Have them perform their dances for each other to the beat of the drum. Each phrase must fill out exactly eight beats—no more, no less. The class evaluates each score.

MULTICULTURAL
CURRICULUM
LESSON PLANS

ANCIENT MESOPOTAMIA

Objectives
To reveal ancient belief systems through early dance forms; to heighten children's awareness of the cultural significance of floor patterns and group formations

Time Allotment
30–45 minutes

Space Requirements
Open space

Materials and Suggested Music
"Chants: Ritual Music" or any earth-centered ritual chanting music; drum; optional: pictures of Mesopotamian artifacts, especially with figures, that include circles, concentric circles, and spirals

Group Format
The whole class together

Lesson Plan

The Circle
Define an area in the room, and ask the children to walk anywhere in that space without touching anyone. When you bang the drum once

they are to stop. Repeat a few times. Then in the same space ask the children to stand in a circle. Direct them to walk around the circle and stop when they hear the drum. Repeat a few times. "How did moving around the space feel different when you could go anywhere and when you had to stay in the circle? Which felt better?" Some students will prefer the restriction of the circle and others the freedom/chaos. Discuss the idea of a circle creating order out of chaos and symbolizing continuity. Why would that be important to ancient Mesopotamian society?

Concentric Circles

Now make a circle with most of the class and put the rest of the children in a smaller inner circle. With hands on each other's shoulders or holding hands, ask them to walk or slowly dance around maintaining their circles. Allow different children to take turns in the inner circle. If there are enough children there can be three concentric circles. "How did you feel being part of the inner circle? How many of you felt protected? How did that feeling compare with being on the outside circle? In which did you feel more protected?" Discuss the idea of concentric circles symbolizing protection.

The Spiral

Starting in one circle again, with everyone holding hands, break the circle in one place taking the *right* hand of the end child and lead the class into a spiral and out again. Music or chanting will help keep everyone moving. Directions: Holding the *right* hand of the child next to you with your *left* hand, you will walk to your *right* going *counterclockwise,* winding into the circle. When you have reached the center with the class wound around you, face the child whose *left* hand you are holding and continue your way out of the circle by passing in *front* of the person holding that child's hand. When you come to the outside of the circle you will be heading *clockwise,* but facing *away* from the center of the circle. You can stay on the outside, with your back to the center, walking until the rest of the class unwinds and is one large circle again, or you can wind your way up again, still with your back to the center. When you get to the center, again pass in *front* of the person whose hand you are holding, and continue your way out of the circle by passing in *front* of the person holding that child's hand. When you come to the outside of the circle this time, you will be walking *counterclockwise again.* Good luck!

You may want to do this spiral a few times, and give some children a chance to be the leader. Ask the class what it felt like when they were in the center of the spiral and how it compared to being on the outside. Discuss the spiral as symbolizing the cycle of birth, death, and rebirth, emphasizing that death in this belief system is not a final end, but rather a stage before rebirth as in the visible cycle of maple trees.

Divide the class into two or three groups to choreograph dances using circles, concentric circles, and spirals. The children can imagine that they are Mesopotamian priests and priestesses performing ancient ritual dances.

NATIVE AMERICAN TRADITIONS AND TALES

Objectives
  I. To explore the significance of the circle and the four directions in Native American traditions
  II. To lead children through a kinesthetic journey honoring animals and dreams
  III. To deepen children's experience of the Pueblo Indian tale *Arrow to the Sun*

Time Allotment
  I. 15–20 minutes
  II and III. Approximately 30 minutes each

Space Requirements
Open space

Materials and Suggested Music
  I. Four fabrics (yellow, red, black, and white), each about five yards long; background music: "Prayer for the Wild Things" by Paul Winter or Native American music
  II. Drum
  III. Four colored fabrics (see I); *Arrow to the Sun,* adapted by Gerald McDermott; drum; Pueblo Indian music such as "Pueblo Songs of the Southwest"

You may want to supplement these lessons with *Indian Sign Language,* by William Tomkins, and with *Dancing Teepees,* edited by Virginia Driving Hawk Sneve.

Group Format
The whole class together

Lesson Plan

I. Set up the fabrics on the floor connecting to each other in a circle according to the directions on the following chart. Ask the children to stand in a circle inside or outside the fabric. "What do you notice about standing in a circle?" (You can see everyone. There's no beginning and no end. We're all connected. No one's left out, etc.) "The circle is very important in many Native American traditions. Some tribes lived in round tepees. Others built their homes in a circle on the land. Many parts of life have a circular connection. Can you name them?" (Seasons, time, life cycle of a seed, water cycle, etc.) Discuss the concept of a modern *time line* versus time as a cycle.

Many Native American tribes assigned different colors and meanings to the four directions of the earth. Using the chart below, face each direction of the circle standing inside or outside of the appropriate color of fabric that describes the circle on the floor. Always maintain the circle (even as you face different directions) as if it represented the Circle of Life. For each direction allow your whole body to move the quality of the symbol (i.e., gentle, light movements; fiery,

Facing south, children dance with fiery gestures

leapy, jumpy movements that stem from the solar plexis; watery, fluid movements like rivers running through your body; strong, large movements grounded in the earth).

DIRECTION	COLOR	SEASON	SYMBOL
East	Yellow	Spring	Light/Peace/Truth/Knowledge
South	Red	Summer	Warmth
West	Black	Autumn	Rains/Rivers/Oceans
North	White	Winter	Wind/Strength/Cold

As they face each direction, children can pantomime associated animals (i.e., eagles for the sky of the eastern sunrise, lizards and snakes for the south, dolphins and whales for the west, polar bear and wolves for the north). You can end this activity sitting in the circle accompanying the following chant with hand motions:

O Great Spirit,
Earth, sun, sky, and sea,
You are inside
And all around me.

II. Instruct children to close their eyes and imagine the earth as a great mother. The flowing rivers are like her blood streams. The mountains and hills follow the curves of her body. The grass and trees are like her hair. Now ask them to open their eyes and begin to walk with this consciousness, not afraid of hurting the earth, but as a baby walks barefoot on its mother's belly. Continue to instruct them with the following story, each child moving freely, silently and independently though the whole class will be moving at the same time. Pause wherever necessary to give children the chance to dance each part of the story:

You are walking barefoot down a wooded path toward a river. You walk through the pine forest with its fresh smells, soft pine needles, and your animal friends. Overhead a hawk circles above the treetops. A little rabbit hops across your trail. You spot a deer through the trees and it freezes, picking up your scent. Suddenly it leaps in the air and darts away. You continue down the path to the bank of the river.

You sit by the edge, splash water on your face, and wiggle yours toes in the river. You're tired, so you lay down and take a nap, and while you sleep, you dream.

In your dream an animal appears to you—it may be a bird, rabbit, turtle, deer, bear, any animal—but something is different about this animal. As it looks deep into your eyes, it begins to speak in its own language, but for the first time ever you *understand* what it is saying. This new friend invites you to follow, and as you do your body begins to take on its shape. The animal leads you to its home, teaches you how to get food, and dances with you in the forest. Then it is time to leave. The animal brings you back to the river bank and whispers a special secret into your ear. Then it disappears into the river.

You wake up and look around. Your animal friend is gone, but you see its tracks leading down to the river. It is time to return to your people. Carefully you retrace your steps through the woods. You spot the deer through the trees and again it freezes, picking up your scent. Suddenly it leaps in the air and darts away. You continue home. A little rabbit hops across your trail. You look up and overhead a hawk circles above the treetops. As you leave the pine forest you see your tribe sitting around a fire, awaiting your return.

Sitting in a circle, the children take turns showing the group their animal, and then showing how their animal dances. Let the rest of the class guess what the animal is. Before rejoining the circle, ask each child to share the special secret of their animal. (Be prepared for some real treasures.)

III. Begin by teaching the children some Native American dance steps that can be put together into a simple circle dance. To give students a sense of the style of dancing, ask them to stand in a circle and imagine that the earth is a drum. "Play the earth drum with your feet. Experiment with rhythms and tempos." This will give them a feel for dancing with a flat foot, as well as a separate ball and heel, rather than our usual way of rolling through the foot heel-ball-toe or toe-ball-heel. Explain also that this dance style is angular, with the body slightly bent at the elbows, hips, and knees. The chest is held proudly high and there is a strong connection to the earth with a small bounce, rather than springing into the air. For instance:

In a circle, facing counterclockwise with left shoulders toward the center, step forward on the right foot ball first, then drop the right heel on the next beat. Repeat on the left foot without changing direction. Continue around the circle, eight steps in all.

Facing toward the center of the circle, step sideways to the right with a flat right foot (toes pointing toward the center of the circle). On the next beat, close the left foot next to the right foot landing with a flat foot. The steps have a subtle bounce. Do this four times as you move sideways around the circle to the right.

Still facing in, shuffle the feet with eight little quick steps as you move in toward the center of the circle. Back out of the circle by stepping back on the right ball of your foot and dropping the right heel on the next beat. Repeat on the left foot. Continue to alternate moving backwards, four steps in all.

Repeat the eight shuffle steps in and four backward ball-heel steps out.

Use this dance as the "Dance of Life" at the end of the story *Arrow to the Sun*.

Preparing the children for the story *Arrow to the Sun:* Set up the fabrics on the floor, connecting to each other in a circle according to the four directions. Children begin the story standing in a circle outside the fabrics. Show them a picture of the pueblo from the book and have them describe what they see, first in words and then with their bodies, connecting to each other with right angles and different levels. Also show them the picture of the Boy (you may wish to use the word *Child* instead of *Boy* to eliminate the perspective of gender), exemplifying the angular quality of the dance style. Describe a *kiva* (underground ceremonial chamber) and divide the students into three groups—wildcats, poisonous snakes, bumble bees. During the story, while each group is performing their animal part inside the *kiva* (inside the circle of fabric), the others are using their bodies to create the walls of the *kiva*. For the final *kiva* of lightning, everyone comes into the center, and the lightning shoots up towards the heavens, so no one gets bumped. The story ends with the circle dance.

Read the book out loud as all the children improvise the story. Pause wherever necessary to give children the chance to dance each section. When the Boy begins the journey, encourage the children to use one of the dance steps. When the Boy comes to the Corn Planter, allow time for the children to do a farming dance showing the cycle of corn and giving thanks back to the earth by planting new kernels. For the Pot Maker children can show the process of shaping, baking, and painting pots. Use your drum to help direct children, and accompany the story with taped Native American music.

KWANZAA

Objectives

To explore the significance of the African-American holiday Kwanzaa; to engage children in a group choreography; to enable children to perceive dance as a way of communicating ideas

Time Allotment

    I. 30 minutes
    II. 45 minutes

Space Requirements

Open space

Materials and Suggested Music

Percussion instruments; any recorded music of master drummer Olatunji; optional: red, green, and black fabric, a basket of whole fruits and vegetables, a video of African dance

Group Format

The whole class together

Lesson Plan

This was inspired by a lesson presented by Dr. Jacqueline Sawyer at a conference of the American Dance Guild in NYC.

I. (For grades K–3)

Explain the history of Kwanzaa as an African American holiday created by Dr. Maulana Karenga in 1966. Though the holiday is observed from December 26–January 1, it actually celebrates the first harvest. (*Kwanzaa* is a Swahili word meaning "first fruit.") Each of the seven days of Kwanzaa represents one of Seven Principles (*Nguzo Saba*) guiding daily living. The idea of community is a central theme of the holiday.

After doing an African dance warm-up, or after watching a video of African dance and doing a warm-up to African music, bring the children into a circle to begin a group creation of a Harvest Dance. The fabrics and fruits can be placed in the center of the circle to inspire the dance. Ask the children to list all the necessary parts of the planting cycle leading to a harvest: removing the rocks, turning the earth, digging holes, planting seeds, rain, sun, weeding, the growing of the plants, the blossoming of the flowers, the growing of the fruit or vegetables, the harvest.

In the proper sequence, have the children improvise movements representing each part of the planting cycle, to the accompaniment of African music. For each part, choose a movement or a combination of movements from the children and have the whole class practice it together. Let the class decide how many times to do it, and whether to do it in place or walking around the circle, going toward the center, or out, etc. Each time you add a new movement, go back to the first and practice the dance up to that point. This will ensure the necessary kinesthetic memory. When the whole dance is choreographed, let children choose percussion instruments to play as they perform the dance. A successful ending could be putting imaginary baskets filled with the harvest on heads and carrying them to market or home, leading students out of the circle.

II. (For grades 4–6)
Explain the holiday of Kwanzaa as in activity I. Discuss each of the Seven Principles and in what ways people can strive to live up to them:

> *Umoja/*Unity
> *Kujichagulia/*Self-determination
> *Ujima/*Collective work and responsibility
> *Ujamaa/*Cooperative economics
> *Nia/*Purpose
> *Kuumba/*Creativity
> *Imani/*Faith

After doing an African dance warm-up, or after watching a video of African dance and doing a warm-up to African music, divide the class into two groups. Working with the spirit of community that is characteristic of Kwanzaa, ask each group to create a dance symbolizing each of the Seven Principles. Provide them with music of African drumming to give them rhythm and energy.

As the groups are working, guide them to select movements that reflect each specific principle. Encourage them to choose group formations which reflect the content of their choreography.

When the groups have rehearsed their finished pieces two times, they can perform for each other and discuss what they have seen.

DESIGN
LESSON PLANS

SHAPE AND DESIGN

Objectives
To help children see the complementary quality of contrast; to encourage children to view sculpture and dance from 360 degrees; to provide children with a structure in which to practice the conversational skills of "listening" and "speaking"

Time Allotment
20–30 minutes

Space Requirements
Open space

Materials and Suggested Music
Drum; Philip Glass or Steve Reich music

Group Format
The whole class together, then in pairs and trios

Lesson Plan

In the format of the freeze game, direct children to create shapes (poses) that are huge, tiny, high level, middle level, low level, rounded, angular, upside down, cavelike, with one leg in the air, etc.

**Contrasting levels in a three-way shape
"conversation"**

After children have experimented with many shapes, ask one child to come in front of the group and make a shape with a lot of spaces in it (legs apart, arms held away from the body), that can be held for a long time. While that child is "frozen" holding the shape, invite another child to come up, and *without touching* the first child, make a shape on a different level, creating a design with the first shape by filling some of the spaces (between the legs, around the torso, under the arms). When the second child freezes in this shape, the first child slips out of the design and makes a new shape on a different level around the second child's shape. As each child freezes, the partner creates a new shape relating to the design of the frozen shape. This is called a "conversation in shape" because no two people are moving at the same time—the way no two people would be speaking at the same time—and each new shape responds to the shape made by the partner. It is, however, a silent, kinesthetic conversation.

Pair up all the children with each set containing an A and a B, and let them have "conversations." At first you can bang your drum to signal the A partner's turn to move. When all the A's are frozen in a shape, bang your drum to signal the B partner's turn. Then A, then B, etc. When the class understands the process, let them change on their own timing, as long as both partners don't move at the same time. Music will help the concentration.

When the partners are comfortable with the exercise and are using contrasting levels and interesting three-dimensional shapes, create new groups of trios. Now you have A, B, and C. The children now have to wait for *two* partners to change shapes before they can move again. Still only one child may move at a time, but the designs and contrasting levels will be more complex. Encourage children to keep their transitional movements minimal, slow, and conscious of shape.

Divide the trios into two groups so that they can watch each other and comment on the timing and designs of each group. You can end with a large group sculpture, each child adding on one at a time.

ARCHITECTURAL PRINCIPLES

Objectives
To help children understand the concepts of weight support and stress points; to introduce children to aesthetic aspects of architecture

Time Allotment
20–30 minutes

Space Requirements
Open space

Materials and Suggested Music
Mats, if possible; any background music

Group Format
Groups of eight to ten children

Lesson Plan

Ask the children to find a variety of ways to hold each other up on at least two levels. Encourage them to experiment using different parts

Experimenting with weight support and stress points

of their body, and bent and straight limbs, to support each other. Discuss their findings for using the least energy to hold the most weight. Point out the greater strength of a straight limb compared to a bent limb. Also, it is more difficult to hold someone standing on the middle of your back when you are on all fours, compared to their standing on your lower back which is above the vertical support of your thigh.

Instruct children to create "body buildings" chosen from the following: open and spacious, closed and tight, tall, wide, full of curves, angular, unusual, funny, scary, etc. Discuss the ornamental aspect of design, where changing the focus of the head or curve of the arms may alter the *feeling* of the structure. The children can also name or title their structures.

As groups display their buildings one at a time, ask the rest of the class to comment on how well the group's goals were achieved and whether they were using the least energy to hold the most weight.

MEDIATION SKILLS AND CONFLICT RESOLUTION LESSON PLANS

THE KNOT

Objectives

To develop skills in cooperative leadership, group problem solving, verbal and nonverbal communication; to encourage positive social integration, accomplishment, acceptance of other perspectives, perseverance, peer empowerment

Time Allotment

15–20 minutes

Space Requirements

Open space

Materials and Suggested Music

Calming music or gentle music

Group Format

Groups of eight to ten children

Lesson Plan

Students stand shoulder to shoulder in a circle in groups of eight to ten. They close their eyes, cross their arms, and reach across the circle. Each hand grabs a hand—one hand per hand—no holding wrists!

Untangling the knot without letting go

Make sure each child is holding hands with *two* other children from across the circle. Students then open their eyes and without letting go of hands, untangle the knot into an open circle (or two).

Repeat the activity, this time without talking! Students can use facial expressions, gestures, and eye contact, but they can't let go of hands!

COMMON GROUND: WIN/WIN SOLUTIONS

Objectives
To help children develop skills in cooperation, observation, synthesis and creative problem solving; to demonstrate many solutions to one problem

Time Allotment
45–60 minutes

Space Requirements
Open space

Materials and Suggested Music
Any music can be used, none is necessary

Group Format
Groups of four

Lesson Plan

Divide students into groups of four. Within each group let children choose who will be *high, low, sustained,* and *percussive.* You may choose other descriptions such as fast and slow, or open and closed. Working individually each student should create a simple, repeatable, teachable movement reflecting his or her description (high, low, sustained, or percussive).

Next have students return to their groups of four. High and low become partners facing each other. Sustained and percussive become partners facing each other. One person from each pair (e.g., high and sustained) repeats her/his movement a few times. Then the other (e.g., low and percussive) answers with her/his own movement. This back and forth can be called a "conversation." Children then learn their partner's movements (high learns low, low learns high; percussive learns sustained, sustained learns percussive).

Each partnership then creates a movement phrase incorporating *both* movements (high and low, or percussive and sustained), which they both perform without losing either of the qualities. Encourage students to use interesting levels and timing.

Both pairs of the group now have a "conversation" with each other using the newly created movement phrases (high/low and sustained/percussive). Each pair then teaches their phrase to the other pair. The group of four now creates a longer phrase incorporating *both* phrases without losing any of the qualities or movements. Again encourage students to use interesting levels and timing. Once all the material is gathered and learned by all four, the group can expand the choreography by using unison, canon form, or contrast, and a variety of floor patterns and group shapes.

Before each group performs its quartet for the whole class, ask to see the four individual movements that were originally choreographed at the beginning of the exercise. Ask the class to evaluate how well the movements were synthesized into the dance without losing their qualities. Discuss the variety of results though each group was given the exact same instructions.

SKILLS FOR MEDIATORS: HUMAN OBSTACLE COURSE

Objectives
To help children develop skills in leadership, communication, and following directions; to encourage attitudes of risk taking, trust, empathy, responsibility, and safety awareness

Time Allotment
30–45 minutes

Space Requirements
Large open space

Materials and Suggested Music
Blindfolds for one-fourth of the class; relaxing music

Group Format
The whole class working together

Lesson Plan

Divide the class into two groups. The first group will create a human obstacle course in groups of one to three children, using only their bodies. The "obstacles" will require people to go over, under, or through them. They can even have moving parts—arms or legs that go up and down, or two people stepping away from and then toward each other—as long as the movement maintains an even tempo and provides enough time for a blindfolded person to pass through.

The second group pairs off into partners, with one child blindfolded and the other designated as the leader. The leader verbally and physically guides the blindfolded partner through the obstacle course. When the last obstacle is passed through, the partners switch roles so that the leader gets blindfolded and the blindfolded one becomes the leader. The obstacle course can make slight alterations to challenge the partners.

Leading blindfolded partners through a human obstacle course

When both partners have completed the course, reverse the groups. New obstacles should be created by the second group.

Allow the children time to discuss with their partners both specific compliments and helpful suggestions as to their leadership and communication skills and how it felt to be guided while blindfolded. Ask them to share the discussions with the whole class. If the class has training in peer mediation, encourage students to identify the applicable mediation skills.

ROLE PLAYING: AVOIDING CONFRONTATION

Objectives
To help children develop skills in communication, group problem solving, and conflict resolution

Time Allotment
30 minutes

Space Requirements
Open space

117
*Mediation Skills
and Conflict
Resolution
Lesson Plans*

Materials and Suggested Music
None

Group Format
Groups of six to ten students

Lesson Plan

Divide the class into groups of six to ten students. Ask each group to set up a frozen scene of a fight about to break out between two students while the rest of the group surrounds them.

Ask each group to choreograph a way to disrupt the fight when the motion begins. Only two nonfighting people can speak and each can only say one sentence during the entire role play. Students should pay particular attention to their spatial arrangements. Possible scenarios (students should fill in the specifics):

a) Everyone in the group is good friends.
b) Everyone in the group is a stranger to each other.
c) The group is composed of two enemy groups.

Each group rehearses the choreography and then performs for the entire class. Ask the students to discuss the verbal and physical ways the fights were disrupted. Discuss different ways to avoid confrontation.

APPENDIX I
Stories That Move Us

These stories for kindergartners have been written to inspire movement. They are intended to be read aloud while children use their bodies to dance/act them out. Encourage the whole group to improvise all of the parts of the story, so that everyone experiences the setting, sequence of events, character development, conflict, and resolution.

Magic Pumpkins

One day a farmer was selling her vegetables in the local market square. Towards the end of the day, an old woman came up and asked if she could have the leftover vegetables that were a little bruised, in exchange for some magic pumpkin seeds. The farmer's heart went out to the old woman. She knew how awful it was to be hungry. And so they exchanged the vegetables for the seeds.

That evening the farmer decided to plant her pumpkin seeds in a big empty field. Slowly, slowly they grew, spreading their roots into the ground and their leaves open to the sun. Soon they sprouted pumpkins . . . little baby pumpkins that grew and grew and grew.

One night when the moon was full and began to rise over the pumpkin field, the pumpkins suddenly turned into jack-o-lanterns. Their eyes popped out and began to glow, their noses popped out, and then their big, broad mouths. Some were smiling and some were scary!

As the moon got higher, the jack-o-lanterns began to rock back and forth, and as they rocked they broke from their vines and began to roll across the field. Then they began sprouting first one arm and then another; then one leg and then another, rolling across the field.

As the moon got higher in the sky the jack-o-lanterns began to dance, some with smiling faces and some with scary faces. First they did jumping dances. And when they got tired of jumping they twirled first one way and then the other. And when they got tired of twirling, they skipped and leaped over the field. They flew through the skies. They had such a good time they got silly and floppy, until one pumpkin pointed to the east and said, "Look! The sun is starting to come up and the moon is starting to go down." And as the sun began to rise, the sky grew lighter and the arms and legs of the jack-o-lanterns grew smaller and smaller until they disappeared. The jack-o-lanterns quickly rolled back across the field to their places on the vines and became pumpkins once more.

That morning after the sun was well high in the sky, the farmer came back to her pumpkin field. She was amazed to see the size of all these full round orange pumpkins. She carefully cut each pumpkin off the vine, gathered them up in her cart, and brought them to market. All the boys and girls in the village came to her cart to see these beautiful pumpkins. They each picked one out and brought it home to set in their windows, on the their tables and porches. They carved unusual faces in the pumpkins, some smiling and some scary, not having any idea that they all had magic pumpkins.

The Musician
This was originally written to be told with a bass player, but any instrument will work with modifications, including a drum.
Way out in a far-off land was a small village, very different from any other village, for in this village lived only children. The children skipped through the streets and twirled through the meadows and rolled down the hills of their little village.

One day, a man appeared in the middle of the biggest pumpkin field, wearing a long, beautiful scarf and carrying a large wooden instrument. He never spoke a word, but he played from early morning until late at night. The children all gathered around him, staring, but no one dared to go close enough to touch him or his instrument. They had never heard such deep, low, beautiful sounds before.

As they listened, their arms began to move, and their heads and bodies and feet, slowly at first, and very smoothly. But as the music got faster, so did the children's dancing. And as the music got jumpier, so did the children's dancing. And as the music got wilder, so did the children's dancing. Until it *stopped* and the children froze like stone statues.

Then the man started to play an eerie, ghostly tune, and the statues started floating through the pumpkin field like thousands of little ghosts barely touching the ground. Again the music stopped and again the children froze like statues. When the man started playing again, deep, low, groaning sounds came from his instrument and the children felt themselves growing bigger and taller until they were huge giants galumphing through the field. Again the music changed: This time it was creaky and squeaky, and the children felt as if the skin dropped off from their bodies and they were nothing but skeletons, bending and twisting and wobbling through the field.

Night started to fall over the pumpkin field, and as the moon rose, the man began to play the sweetest most beautiful music the children had ever heard. In slow motion, as if time had stopped, the children slowly began to dance toward the musician and circle around him, lifting their arms high and then bowing down ever so low, almost like horses on a carousel. Finally the music stopped, and the children stopped in mid-motion, frozen again like statues of stone. Then the man lifted his bow high in the air, and all the statues melted slowly to the ground. They curled up into tight little pumpkin shapes, closed their eyes, and fell fast asleep.

They slept all that night and late into the next morning. When they awoke they stretched and yawned and looked about. All they saw was each other. They wondered how it came to be that they were sleeping in the pumpkin field. No one remembered how they got there. No one remembered the musician. No one remembered anything about the night before. Then someone noticed an unusual colored scarf lying in the middle of the pumpkin field. They hung it up in a doorway to see if anyone could remember where it came from. But no one ever remembered while they were awake. Only when they slept did they visit the musician again in their dreams.

The Apple Tree
This is based on a story my cousin used to tell my children. Before you begin telling this story, cut an apple in half laterally.
Many years ago on a grassy hillside, a farmer decided to plant some apple trees. The trees grew into fine sturdy trees with wonderfully twisted branches that hung low with the weight of juicy red apples which fell to the ground and rolled down the hill.

One day a child was climbing up the hill and spotted a huge, shiny apple. The child plucked the apple, and continued to the top of the hill. There the child ate the crisp fruit and buried the core in the moist warm earth.

Weeks passed, and under the ground tiny roots sprouted from the seed. One day a tiny little green shoot pushed its head up through the earth reaching for the sun. Two little green leaves appeared. Week after week it grew taller and stronger. Month after month the stalk grew thicker. Year after year it became a beautiful twisted apple tree.

Each spring the apple tree's beautiful pink blossoms would float down and cover the ground like a soft blanket. And in place of the blossoms, little round apples would begin to grow, and get rounder and bigger, rounder and bigger, day by day. When the apples fell off and rolled down the hill, the leaves from the tree would blow away in gusts on the autumn wind. By winter the tree would stand bare and reach its twisted arms up to the cold grey sky.

But no matter what the season, the tree always spent the night admiring the twinkling stars. Sometimes there would be a shooting star streaking through the sky. Sometimes the stars would look like pictures called constellations. One time the tree saw a swan made out of stars, another time a giant "W" like a huge throne, a lion, a bear, even a hunter. The tree wished more than anything that it could have stars hanging from its branches.

One night as the tree was gazing at the shining stars, it fell asleep and dreamt that all the stars of the sky started moving about, gliding here and there across the night sky. The stars began to zip and fly quicker and wilder through the sky until suddenly there was a great burst and a huge flower of fireworks. In slow motion they drifted and floated through the air until they landed softly and gently on the branches of the apple tree. The wind blew a soft breeze whispering, "Now you are filled with stars, now you are filled with stars." And as the tree swayed in the breeze it slowly woke up. As the tree remembered its dream, it shuddered, and the largest of its apples fell to the ground and cracked in half. The tree's heart began to swell with joy for there in the center of this wonderful apple, was a perfect star. *[Teacher shows cut apple halves revealing stars.]* The tree's wish had come true. Now it knew that hanging from its branches were stars.

Just like the tree had stars inside of its apples, so too does every person have something very special, their own shining star, inside of them. As you grow up, it is up to each of you to discover what that specialness is.

The Ice Fairies

This story takes place in the same magic land in the small village where only children lived. This time it is in the middle of a very cold winter.

One morning as the children stretched and yawned as they rolled out of bed, they heard a terrible snowstorm howling outside. After eating some warm cereal and drinking hot cocoa, they dressed themselves up in snowpants, boots, sweaters, bright colored jackets, hats, mittens, and, finally, wound warm woolen scarves around their necks. They could hardly move being bundled up so, but they tramped outside into the deep snow.

The snow was whirling about in a terrible blizzard, tossing the children this way and that. It was so blinding they couldn't see their own hands in front of their faces. Frozen and shivering, the children made their way back inside and unbundled their scarves, mittens, hats, bright colored jackets, sweaters, boots, and snowpants, and warmed themselves by the fire. The fire was hot and blazing with curvy blue shapes and pointy orange ones.

Softly at first, and then louder, the children started to hear a voice singing to them from outside. It was a most beautiful voice that sounded like chiming glass bells, and it sang:

> Come on children, come outside
> Dance with the fairies—slip and slide
> Come on children, come outside
> Dance with the fairies—slip and slide.

At first the children tried to ignore it, but the voice was so beautiful, and they wanted to see the fairies, so they got all bundled up again. Snowpants, boots, sweaters, bright colored jackets, hats, mittens, and, finally, they wound warm woolen scarves around their necks. Outside the beautiful voice sang:

> Come to the snowy meadow with me
> That's where the dancing fairies will be.

The children trudged their way through the blinding windy blizzard until they came to the big open field covered with glistening snow. It was calmer there, and dancing round and round, leaving no footprints, were beautiful boy and girl fairies, their wings dusted with snow flakes and icicles shining in their hair. The voice said:

> Remember—go home when the sun goes down
> Or you will be wearing an icicle gown.

The fairies held out their hands to the children asking them to join, but the children huddled together, afraid to go closer. Finally one little girl cautiously crept up to a fairy with long flowing hair and reached out her hand. As soon as she touched the fairy, all her winter clothes disappeared. There she was dressed for summer and she wasn't cold at all! The wind became a soft breeze, and the snow like fairy dust. Even the sun seemed to shine in her hair. One by one the children began to join the circle, and as each child took someone's hand, all their winter clothes disappeared and they too felt warm and sunny. The fairies started to dance again.

> Skipping this way round and round
> Skipping that way off the ground
> Clapping hands (one two three)
> Clap your feet (just follow me)
> Slipping sliding here and there
> Spinning twirling everywhere
> Leaping, gliding through the air.

The children were having such a good time they didn't notice that the sun was beginning to set, that the full moon was starting to rise. The voice started singing again:

> Run home children the sun's going down
> Or soon you'll be wearing an icicle gown.

But the children kept on dancing with the ice fairies.

> Skipping this way round and round
> Skipping that way off the ground
> Clapping hands (one two three)
> Clap your feet (just follow me)
> Slipping sliding here and there
> Spinning twirling everywhere
> Leaping, gliding through the air.

One little boy finally realized what was going to happen and he ran out of the circle. Suddenly all his winter clothes were on him again. He felt the cold wind bite his cheeks and the cold snow freeze his fingers. When the other children saw what happened to him, they remembered where they really were, and they too ran out of the circle into the cold and became suddenly dressed in their bright colored snowsuits.

Only the first little girl to join the fairies did not leave. She would not stop dancing the fairy dance. The other children called to her and pleaded. But she would not come. The sky was growing darker, the moon was getting higher. Suddenly the wind stopped. The fairies disappeared and the little girl became frozen into an ice statue in the middle of her dance. She didn't move. No sound came from the glistening ice statue. The children were frightened. One child put her jacket over the ice child, another put his hat on her head. A third gave her his mittens. Slowly they trudged their way back home. It was late and they were very tired. No one was very hungry. After sipping some warm tea, the children went to bed.

Next morning, the storm was long gone. The sun was shining. All the children awoke early and ran out to the meadow to see what had become of the little girl turned to ice. There in the middle of the meadow was no longer an ice statue, but a marble statue of a fairy, white and shiny, posed so lifelike in a dance of joy. This kind fairy had seen one tear dripping down the cheek of the frozen child. She had changed places with her so that the little girl could live. Sitting in the snow at the base of the statue, looking up at the frozen fairy, was the child.

The statue never turned back into a live fairy, and it remained forever in the meadow to remind the children of that mysterious day. Never again did they hear that beautiful voice. Never again did the ice fairies return. But every year in the middle of the winter, the marble statue would turn to ice for one night under the full moon.

APPENDIX II
Suggested Music to Accompany Kinesthetic Lessons

Warm-up and friendly music:

The Great Ragtime Classics
Paul Hersh and David Montgomery, Pianists
RCA Victrola ALK1-9543

Street Song—"Gassenhauer"
Carl Orff
Quintessence P4C-7127
(great for children; can be used for anything)

Bach: Goldberg Variations
Glenn Gould, piano
CBS Records MYK 38479

Gentle background music/meditative:

Prayer for the Wild Things
Paul Winter
Earth Music Productions LD0028
PO Box 68
Litchfield, CT 06759

Music of Samuel Barber
Adagio for Strings
The Vox Music Group/Essex Entertainment CDX 5091

Holst: The Planets
"Saturn"
London Symphony Orchestra
LaserLight 14 010

Nonspecific energizing music:

Music for Mallet Instruments, Voices and Organ
Steve Reich
Elektra Nonesuch 9 79220-2

Baka
Outback (name of the group)
Rykodisc HNCD 1357
Pickering Wharf, Bldg. C
Salem, MA 01970
(great Australian music that makes you want to dance)

Good story music:

Schubert: Quintet D.956 (Adagio)
Juilliard String Quartet
CBS Records/Masterworks MK 42383

Underground Railroad:

All for Freedom
Sweet Honey in the Rock
Music for Little People MLP 2230
PO Box 1460
Redway, CA 95560

Music and the Underground Railroad
The Kim and Reggie Harris Group
Ascension Records KRH 002
Box 18871
Philadelphia, PA 19119

African music:

Drums of Passion: The Invocation
Olatunji
RYKODISC RACS 0102
(West African master drummer)

Best of Ladysmith Black Mambazo
Shanachie 43098
(famous South African a cappella group)

Native American music:

Pueblo Songs of the Southwest
Recorded live at the 48th Inter-Tribal Ceremonial
1969, Gallup, New Mexico
Indian House IH 9502-C

Massacre
Muskwachees, Vol. 5
ARS 550

Ritual chant music:

Chants: Ritual Music
Reclaiming Chants
PO Box 14404
San Francisco, CA 94114

Other:

Kronos Quartet Performs Philip Glass
Nonesuch 79356-2

APPENDIX III
Suggested Reading

Andrews, Gladys. 1976. *Creative Rhythmic Movement: Boys and Girls Dancing*. Englewood Cliffs, NJ: Prentice-Hall.

Bagley, Michael, and Karen Hess. 1987. *Two Hundred Ways of Using Imagery in the Classroom*. New York: Trillium Press.

Bellanca, James, and Robin Fogarty. 1991. *Blueprints for Thinking in the Cooperative Classroom*. Palatine, IL: Skylight Publishing.

Benzwie, Teresa. 1987. *A Moving Experience*. Tucson, AZ: Zephyr Press.

Blatt, Gloria, and Jean Cunningham. 1981. *It's Your Move: Expressive Movement Activities for the Language Arts Class*. New York: Teachers College Press.

Bloom, Benjamin S. 1984, reprint. *Taxonomy of Educational Objectives*. Handbook I: Cognitive Domain. New York: Longman.

Edwards, Carolyn, George Forman, and Lella Gandini, eds. 1993. *The Hundred Languages of Children: The Reggio Emilia Approach to Early Childhood Education*. Greenwich, CT: Ablex.

Gallas, Karen. 1994. *The Languages of Learning*. New York: Teachers College Press .

Gardner, Howard. 1983. *Frames of Mind*. New York: HarperCollins.

———. 1993. *Multiple Intelligences: The Theory in Practice*. New York: HarperCollins.

Gilbert, Anne Green. 1977. *Teaching the Three R's Through Movement Experiences*. Minneapolis: Burgess Publishing.

Graham, Martha. 1991. *Blood Memory*. New York: Doubleday.

Gregory, Cynde. 1990. *Childmade: Awakening Children to Creative Writing*. New York: Station Hill Press.

Joyce, Mary. 1973. *First Steps in Teaching Creative Dance*. Palo Alto, CA: Mayfield Publishing.

Levine, Mindy, and Elizabeth Zimmer. 1987. *Dance: A Social Study*. New York: ArtsConnection.

Sachs, Curt. 1937. *World History of the Dance*. New York: W. W. Norton & Co.

Tomkins, William. 1969. *Indian Sign Language*. New York: Dover.

Williams, Harriet. 1983. *Perceptual and Motor Development*. Englewood Cliffs, NJ: Prentice-Hall.

Children's Books, K–5

Arnott, Kathleen. 1990. *African Myths and Legends*. New York: Oxford University Press. See especially "The Calabash Children."

Brown, Marcia. 1982. *Shadow*. New York: Charles Scribner's Sons.

Carle, Eric. 1987. *The Tiny Seed*. New York: Scholastic.

———. 1989. *Animals, Animals*. New York: Scholastic.

Goble, Paul. 1978. *The Girl Who Loved Wild Horses*. New York: Simon and Schuster.

Hudson, Wade. 1993. *Pass It On: African-American Poetry for Children*. New York: Scholastic.

McDermott, Gerald. 1974. *Arrow to the Sun*. New York: Viking.

Medearis, Angela Shelf. 1991. *Dancing with the Indians*. New York: Scholastic.

Lionni, Leo. 1963. *Swimmy*. New York: Knopf.

Lobel, Arnold. 1968. *The Great Blueness*. New York: Harper & Row.

MacDonald, Golden. 1946, 1974. *The Little Island*. New York: Scholastic.

Prelutsky, Jack, ed. 1983. *The Random House Book of Poetry for Children*. New York: Random House.

Price, Christine. 1979. *Dance on the Dusty Earth*. New York: Charles Scribner's Sons.

Seeger, Pete. 1986. *Abiyoyo*. New York: MacMillan.

Segal, Edith. 1952. *Be My Friend*. Secaucus, NJ: Citadel Press.

Sendak, Maurice. 1963. *Where the Wild Things Are*. New York: Scholastic.

Seuss, Dr. [Theodore Geiser]. 1971. *The Lorax*. New York: Random House.

Shannon George. 1982. *Dance Away.* New York: Mulberry Books.

Sneve, Virginia Driving Hawk, ed. 1989. *Dancing Teepees.* New York: Holiday House.

Stevenson, Robert Louis. 1929. *A Child's Garden of Verses.* New York: Platt and Munk Co.

UNICEF, ed. 1993. *I dream of peace.* New York: HarperCollins Publishers.

White Deer of Autumn. 1991. *Ceremony—In the Circle of Life.* Hillsboro, OR: Beyond Words Publishing.

Winter, Jeanette. 1988. *Follow the Drinking Gourd.* New York: Knopf.